How to Become a
Mental Millionaire

J. Martin Kohe

TABLE OF CONTENTS

CHAPTER 1

GETTING READY FOR SUCCESS

Congratulations . . . by starting to read this book you have just taken the first step toward becoming a Mental Millionaire. Do your realize that you and I, at this very moment and time, have a lot in common? We are human beings created in the image of Almighty God. We speak and read the same language. We enjoy many of the same foods. We've probably visited many of the same cities with their historical sights and various points of interest. But above and beyond that, we both want to enjoy a more successful, happy, enriched life--regardless of the levels of success, happiness and enrichment we have experienced up to this point in our lives.

You probably purchased this book for several reasons. You wanted to improve yourself and your self-image, you wanted to gain more self-confidence, you wanted more peace of mind, and you want to get more zest out of living. In short, you want to obtain the very best this life has to offer and capitalize upon it to its fullest extent. You may want to kick the fear and worry habit, you may want to increase your personal income, you may want to be more at ease with yourself and other people. I'm sure you have a burning desire to be a better doctor, a better lawyer, a better salesman, a better truck driver, a better housewife, a better husband, a better Christian-- a better something! In essence, you want to become a mental millionaire, and with the help of this book, you create a plan of action that will assist you in achieving that goal.

Let me share with you a very profound point. What you read in this book may not be anything new to you . . . no startling new discoveries . . . no amazing solutions . . . no creative theories . . . but what you will discover is that you can take a great deal of the knowledge which you now possess and build it into a system that will literally produce a miracle within your life. Many of the principles I will share with you in this book are very old. As a matter of fact, many of the principles can be found expressed in different ways in the Holy Bible. For example, Matthew 5 tells us that we are the salt of the earth, the light of the world, and we should let our light so shine before men that they may see our good works. Jesus is telling you that you are worthy and valuable and that you should use your talents to their fullest extent. Even though you have known this for some time, for some reason that concept just hasn't seemed to work out for you in the past. But keep this in mind . . . you may have been trying to attain those goals through knowledge and education . . . but successful and meaningful education isn't just knowledge . . . it's also our attitudes put into action. To **know** you are the salt of the earth is a lot different than providing savor to the earth. To **know** you are the light of the world is a lot different than letting your light shine. You must have the education and knowledge first, and then that acquired knowledge must be put into action if it is to be meaningful and useful.

Therefore, I want you to remember . . . your success in life, from this moment on, is going to depend not so much on WHAT you know, but on how well you PRACTICE what you know.

Look at your daily life. You get paid for what you put into practice. In our consulting firm, it's not just enough for Jim Cavanaugh and Ken Link to possess knowledge, that knowledge must be placed into pragmatic, successful actions in order for our clients to become more efficient and effective in their operations. The lawyer earns his living by taking the knowledge he has acquired in Law School and applying it to meet specific needs and legalities. The doctor has acquired knowledge concerning your physical body and its specific needs and he gets paid for putting that knowledge into practice by making you well when you are sick. The teachers in our educational systems have acquired a great deal of knowledge and, like the attorney or the doctor, they are paid for putting that knowledge into practice. They share their ideas, their concepts, their philosophies with their students in order that the students might also learn. So this is a fundamental key to life--we get paid for what we put into practice! The more you motivate yourself to accomplish your plan through action, the bigger the reward. That is just one of the basic laws of life that you must understand and believe.

If you'll take the time, effort, and energy to utilize the principles, systems, and Plans of Action outlined in this book, you will not only gain knowledge which you can put into practice but you will also end up getting MORE LIVING OUT OF LIFE AND MORE LIFE OUT OF LIVING.

We live in a golden age. This is an era that men and women have looked forward to, have dreamed of, have worked toward for thousands of years. But now that it's here, unfortunately, we have a tendency to take it for granted. Maybe that's partly the cause of many of our present day problems. Ours is a land of abundant opportunity for everyone . . . not just a select few. For **everyone** that is willing to exert the energy to acquire knowledge and put that knowledge into practice through action. But you know what happens to too many people? Taking a look at one hundred individuals who start out at the age of twenty, and asking any one of them if they want to be successful in life, they would tell you they surely do want to be successful. One of their greatest goals is to be successful in their chosen profession. As you observe them, you'll notice they have an eagerness toward life! There's a sparkle in their eyes! There's an erectness in their carriage, and life seems very interesting and challenging to them! But, unfortunately, by the time these one hundred individuals have reached the age of 65, only **five** of them will have achieved the goal of being successful in terms of how they originally perceived success. Only 5% will have achieved the goal of success in the greatest, most successful, land in the world.

What is success? Success is the progressive realization of what you perceive to be a worthy ideal. It's amazing that we learn to read by the time we are seven . . . we learn to make a living by the time we are twenty-five, and usually we have a family half-raised by the time we reach thirty years of age . . . and yet by the time we are sixty-five, the great majority of Americans haven't learned how to be financially independent in the richest land in the world, even though their earnings may well have exceeded one million dollars during their lifetime. That's just $25,000 a year for a period of forty years. But more important than that . . . only two out of that one hundred will have learned the real art of living a successful and happy life. Why only 2%? Because that 2% did not conform to the routine philosophies of the other 98%. They developed the philosophy of becoming a mental millionaire . . . of getting more living out of life and more life out of living.

They realized that life is composed of what I call a Triple "A" philosophy . . . Attitude plus Action plus Altitude. Our attitude is our frame of mind, or our sense of values. Our actions are a direct result of our attitude. And our altitude is our personal relationship with Almighty God. It is the ability to really believe we are the salt of the earth, and the light of the world, and that we do have within us the talents, abilities, and capabilities to let our lights so shine before men that they may see our good works.

You do have within you the ability to be extremely successful. That's why this book challenges every one of you to start right now and prepare for success. Be willing to set your mind on goals that are worthy ideals. Be willing to commit yourself to be a part of that 2% that gets the most out of life. If you're not committed to something, you will fall for anything.

Phillip Brooks once said, "Do not pray for tasks equal to your power, but pray for power equal to your tasks." I think Jesus illustrated this point very clearly in Matthew 25:14 when He talked about the parable of the talents. One man was given five talents, another two, another one. The man who was given five talents had the power, ambition and desire to meet the task of earning another five talents. The man who was given two talents also met his task by earning another two talents. But the man who had only one talent obviously did not pray for the power necessary to meet the task of equaling that one talent, so he buried it. As a result, his punishment was great, and he was cast into darkness. The man with the five talents and the man with the two talents had the proper attitude and perception about their task. I learned a long time ago that life is 10% what you make it, and 90% how you take it. Your perception on how you see the world is so important. Is the glass half full, or is it half empty? Have you paid half the debt, or do you have half the debt yet to pay?

I'm reminded of the story of the young boy from Missouri who learned the true art of perception. He said, "When I was a young boy growing up, my father used to say to me, 'Listen, stupid.' He always called me 'Listen'." The boy had learned a secret to life. Life is 10% what you make it and 90% how you take it!

William James, the father of American philosophy, said, "The greatest discovery of my generation is that we have learned we can alter our lives by altering our attitudes of mind." Think about that . . . We can alter our **lives** by altering our **attitudes** of mind! Life is 10% what you make it . . . 90% how you take it. That's a secret to life you must understand and accept as you get ready for success.

One principle philosophers of all ages have agreed upon is that we become what we think about. Solomon put it very simply in the Bible when he said, "As a man thinketh in his heart, so is he." A dream remains a dream until our thought processes are filled with so much concentration that we start doing something to achieve that dream. At that point, the dream will become a reality. Someone once said, "The greatest room in the world is the room for self-improvement." Regardless of our level of successful achievement, we all have room for self-improvement.

You and I have but one life to live, so let me challenge you to start living that life to its fullest potential right now. Don't delay . . . don't procrastinate . . . start right now with a commitment. Get ready for success! There is no special age requirement for success. So forget that excuse. Don't say, "I'm too young" . . . or, "I'm too old" . . . or, "It's not time" . . . or, "I'll start later." Start succeeding right now! You are at the right age, be it 16 or 65. Regardless of your age, get ready for success--right now!

You are encouraged to place upon yourself a great deal of self-discipline . . . because as you get ready for success, you'll discover that your self-discipline begins with your thoughts. Self-discipline is an important requirement for individual success and it yields the most satisfactory results. It is through the power of self-discipline that you can balance the emotions of the heart with the reasoning of the mind to achieve your goal and objective. The person controlling himself through self-discipline can never be controlled by others. One thing is certain in this life . . . you will either control your environment or your enviroment will control you.

Let me pause here for just a moment. You might be saying to yourself at this very instant, "This all sounds good, but I've tried this type of thinking before and it never worked out for me." But, the chances are you have never taken your thoughts and ideas and built them into a system that will work. In this book, we're going to share with you the various systems and plans of action that will cause you to become a mental millionaire.

Let me ask you a very personal question as you are getting ready for success. How do you know you can't be successful until you have attempted it one more time? You don't, do you? Isn't it worth that extra effort . . . isn't it worth going that extra mile . . . isn't it worth trying one more time to get more living out of life and more life out of living? Certainly it's worth it for the rewards far out-distance the effort.

Someone once said that life is a four-letter word. The middle two letters being "if". The "if" depends upon you! If your mental attitudes are right . . . if your actions are alive . . . if your systems are consistent . . . if your abilities are utilized to their fullest extent . . . then you will become a mental millionaire. If we take the "if" out of life, that leaves us with an L and an E, which stand for "learning" and "experience". When you put your Attitudes, Actions and Abilities along with your Learning and Experiencing new concepts, you're on your way to a new life you never dreamed possible.

For a start, take a pencil and a piece of paper and write down **what you really want out of life.** What are the things you would like to achieve? Make that list, and then come back and continue reading.

Maybe you wrote that you would like to have a better outlook on life. Maybe you wrote that you would like to make more money. Maybe you wrote that you'd like to have a better job, or get a promotion in your present job. Maybe you wrote that you would like to lose weight. All of the things which you wrote you'd obviously like to achieve and, of course, everybody wants to improve themselves. But, amazingly enough, 98% of the people don't really know HOW. They don't know what to do to earn that pay raise, or to receive that promotion, or to get a better outlook on life, or how to lose weight, or to create the right mental attitudes necessary to succeed. They may have written something down, but they don't have the system to follow through to success. They either don't know, or else they don't apply what they do know. The vast majority of people in the world today have everything just backwards. They go about it entirely wrong. They believe that you GET and then you GIVE. That is simply not true. You GIVE and then you GET. Jesus taught this concept years ago, and yet most people still haven't comprehended that message after 2000 years.

In this book we will discuss how you can achieve more benefits from your job, your family, your marriage, and end up getting more excitement out of life. It's a way that's foolproof and one that will work for you almost 100% of the time. It's as natural as the law of gravity. It will work for you whether you're a self-employed executive, a pencil salesman, an iron worker, a garbage collector, a housewife, a preacher . . . whatever. It will work for you if you will work for it! There's an old saying that remains so true even today. "Plan your work, and work your plan." There are a lot of people in the world today who spend a lot of time planning their work, but then they fail to go the extra mile and work their plan. The formula is so obvious that some people may scoff at it and pass it off as being too simple or too ivory-towered for them to apply to their system of life. But don't sell it short, or you'll rob yourself of the benefits that it will surely bring you if you apply it in your daily living. The secret formula of which I am speaking is simply this . . . we must learn to go the extra mile. We must learn to do more than is expected of us. We can't become a mental millionaire by just thinking. I believe strongly in the power of positive thinking, but there's more to it than that. The system includes **thinking and acting.** It is easier to **act** yourself into a new way of thinking than it is to **think** yourself into a new way of acting.

Did you ever watch a small child trying to learn the process of tying a shoelace? That child could think forever about tying that shoelace, but until he started the process of action . . . until he went through the painful, agonizing experience of trying time and time again to tie that shoelace into a bow, he would never have succeeded. But by thinking AND acting . . . by doing . . . he succeeded. Therefore, you must act yourself into a new way of thinking rather than trying to think yourself into a new way of acting.

How many times have you thought about losing weight? You thought . . . and you thought . . . and you thought . . . and you never got the job done. As a matter of fact, you might even have gained a pound or two. But isn't it amazing that the moment you start to act, the moment you start to eat the foods necessary for a proper diet, you start to lose weight. You start to feel better. As a result, you start to create a new, positive self-image. Why? Because you're acting yourself into a new way of thinking about eating, instead of thinking about a new way of eating and not acting.

You may be thinking, "That's no secret. Jesus talked about that same philosophy 2000 years ago as he expressed the keys to Christianity and Christian living." You're absolutely right. But, unfortunately, many of us do not follow His simple example. We have been hoodwinked into believing we can think ourselves into a new way of life, while the key is we must act ourselves into new ways of thinking. Successful people **do** apply this principle, while failures never seem to merit nor benefit from the facts that this concept brings to us.

Why do you think Henry Ford and Thomas Edison and Walt Disney were such tremendous successes? It's because they went the extra mile . . . they were more than just thinkers. They were doers! But they were also givers. They gave the world more than they took from it. "Yes, but look at what the world gave them!" The world gave to them only after they had given to the world first. The degree of their success was in direct proportion to their contributions to the world. Your's will be too. That's the law. You can't contribute to the pleasure, enjoyment, and the success of others without making your own life more pleasureful, enjoyable, and successful.

Edwin Markham expressed this truth in his poem, **The Creed.**

There is a destiny that makes us brothers
None goes his way alone.
All that he sends into the lives of others
Comes back into his own.

At this point I would like to encourage all of you to accept what I believe to be a truism of life. You may create the right attitudes and the right physical actions, but the situations will not always work out exactly as you want them to, even if you follow the principles of this book to the letter. You can't always expect to be on the mountaintop. God illustrated this to us very clearly in his creation when He created two valleys for every mountaintop. Life is like licking honey off a thorn. The sweetness is divine, but occasionally we're going to feel some pain and agony in achieving that sweetness. No difficulties--no discoveries. No pains--no gains. Remember what I said earlier--part of life is learning and experiencing. But the key to becoming a Mental Millionaire is your ability to ride high during those times when others would fall low. Maybe this poem illustrates it more clearly . . .

It's easy to be pleasant
When life flows like a song.
But the man worthwhile
Is the one who'll smile
When everything goes dead wrong.

For the test of the heart is trouble,
And it always comes with the years.

> And the smile that is worth the praises
> of earth
> Is the smile that shines through the tears.

You have already started to develop a philosophy that will assist you in riding over those rough times of life. A secret to always remember is that defeat isn't bitter if you don't swallow it. The problem is that 98% of the people in the world swallow that defeat, and then they complain about the bitter taste in their mouths.

Everything that happens to us in life can be used for self-development if we have created the proper mental attitude.

> If you want to be happy begin where
> you are.
> Don't wait for some rapture that's future
> or far.
> Begin to be joyous. Begin to be glad.
> And soon you'll forget thet you ever
> were sad.

There was a popular song back in the 40's that said, "You've got to accentuate the positive and eliminate the negative." How true that is! While you are preparing for success, remember you must learn the art of acting out your thoughts while accentuating the positives in order to eliminate the negatives. Thousands of people today spend too much time accentuating the negative side of life. They spend too much time in worry rather than spending their time in constructive solutions to the problems they're worrying about. In Chapter 7 we will discuss problem-solving, and share some ideas that can be of tremendous value to you.

But why worry? Worry is like a rocking chair. It keeps you busy and gets you nowhere. This little poem expresses that feeling so well . . .

> Worry never climbed a hill.
> Worry never paid a bill.
> Worry never dried a tear.
> Worry never calmed a fear.
> Worry never darned a heel.
> Worry never cooked a meal.
> Worry never led a horse to water.
> Worry never did a thing you thought it oughter.

Realistically, it simply does no good to worry. Spend your valuable time developing the right mental attitude that will help you reach solutions to your problems rather than just living with the problems you have.

As you start developing the attitudes which will make you a Mental Millionaire, remember there are four keys to success, and these will be interspersed throughout this book. They are . . .

> Involvement
> Investigation
> Experience
> Discovery

You have started with involvement by simply

holding this book in your hands. As you read, you're going to investigate certain new ideas, new concepts, new beliefs, new insights. You will go out and experience those new ideas, concepts, beliefs, and thoughts, and as you experience them, you're going to discover it is possible for you to become a Mental Millionaire. You are going to discover that you are getting more living out of life and more life out of living. You are going to discover it's a lot more fun to spread sunshine than doom and gloom.

> The man who deals in sunshine
> Is the man who wins the crowds.
> He does a lot more business
> Than the man who peddles clouds.

I do hope that's one of the philosophies you will have accepted as you're getting ready for success. If not, you need to adopt it very quickly because it will help you become a Mental Millionaire. One of the greatest philosophies you can develop is one that spreads sunshine throughout the world.

As mentioned earlier, this book will probably only touch 2% of you that read it. The other 98% will read it, think it's fine, lay it down, and unfortunately, forget it. For that 2%, it will change their lives and make them successful. For the other 98%, unfortunately, they will continue spending a great deal of time conforming, then being very unhappy about the conformations which they have made.

I think the Holy Bible made the point of conforming very clear to all of us. The writer of the 12th chapter of Romans is talking about a spiritual aspect, but I think the concept is also true and applies to us in our successful patterns and actions of life. The Bible says, "Be not conformed to this world, but be ye transformed by a renewing of your mind."

Unfortunately, one of the patterns of behavior many people have a tendency to develop is the pattern of conformity. Avoid it like the plague! Conformity is so well illustrated by a poem written by Sam Walter Foss, entitled **The Calf Path**. After you have read this poem, I want you to promise yourself you will never again fall into the pattern so clearly illustrated here.

> One day through the primeval wood
> A calf walked home as good calves should.
> And made a trail all bent askew
> A crooked trail as all calves do.
>
> Since then three hundred years have fled
> And I infer that calf is dead.
> But still he left behind his trail
> And thereby hangs my moral tale.
>
> The trail was taken up next day
> By a lone dog that passed that way.
> And then a wise bellwether sheep
> Pursued the trail o'er vale and steep.
>
> And drew the flock behind him too
> As good bellwethers always do.

And from that day o'er hill and glade
Through those old woods a path was made.

And many men wound in and out,
And dodged and turned and bent about.
And uttered words of righteous wrath
Because 'twas such a crooked path.

But still they followed, do not laugh,
The first migrations of that calf.
And through this winding woodway
stalked
Because he wobbled when he walked.

This forest path became a lane
That bent and turned and turned again.
This crooked lane became a road
Where many a poor horse with his load
Toiled on beneath the burning sun
And traveled some three miles in one.

And thus a century and a half
They trod the footsteps of that calf.
The years passed on in swiftness fleet
The road became a village street.
And this before men were aware,
A city's crowded thoroughfare.

And soon the central street was this
Of a renown metropolis.
And men two centuries and a half
Trod in the footsteps of that calf.

Each day a hundred thousand route
Follow this zig zag calf about.
And o'er his crooked journey went
The traffic of a continent.

A hundred thousand men were led
By one calf near three centuries dead.
They followed still his crooked way
And lost one hundred years a day.

And thus such reverence is lent
To well established precedent.
A moral lesson this might teach
Were I ordained and called to preach.

For men are prone to go it blind,
Along the calf path of the mind.
And work away from sun to sun
To do what other men have done.

They follow in the beaten track
And out and in and forth and back.
And still their devious course pursue
To keep the path that others do.

They kept the path a sacred groove
Along which all their lives they move.
But how the wise old wood gods laugh
Who saw the first primeval calf.

Oh many things this tale might teach,
But I am not ordained to preach.

Many of you have lived your lives following

the calf-path of the mind already established by others. Now that you have started down a new road of getting ready to succeed, I encourage you to stand strong, and absorb the realization that life will hold more for you in the future than it has in the past. You really are the salt of the earth. You really are the light of the world. The time has come for you to let your light so shine before men that they may see your good works and indeed you glorify our Father which is in heaven.

Thomas Wolfe said, ". . . to every man a chance. To every man, regardless of his birth, a shining golden opportunity. To every man the right to live, to work, to be himself, and to become whatever his manhood and vision can combine to make him . . . ".

You have now started on your road to success. You deserve a chance, regardless of your birth. You deserve a shining golden opportunity, regardless of your past. You deserve the right to live, to work, and to be yourself. In short, you deserve success--expect nothing less. Get ready for success, because success is ready for you!

CHAPTER 2

TAKING A LOOK AT YOURSELF

*"But ye are a chosen generation, a
royal priesthood and holy nation,
a peculiar people; that ye should
shew forth the praises of Him who
hath called you out of darkness
into His marvelous light."*
                                        1 Peter 2:9

What do you think of yourself? Sounds like
a simple enough question. Yet the importance
of your answer is staggering. What you think
of yourself determines to a large extent what
you are going to achieve in life. It has been
proven time and time again that you will not
rise above the self-image concepts you have.
You act out what you believe yourself capable
of performing. You, yourself, set the limits
and determine the areas and perimeters of your
personal accomplishments. It would be foolish
not to realize that ability, "I.Q.", breaks, and
even luck, may play a part in your achievements.
But in the long run, none of these are as important as the mental picture you have of yourself. While the "I.Q." is important, it is not
nearly as important as the "I Will."

Why do some people become bank presidents
while other accept a career of sweeping the
floor? Why do some people collect rare art
while others collect garbage? Why do some
students make A's, and others with equal ability
just get by? The answer is found in what we
call "self-perception" . . . the way you see your-

self . . . the way you feel about yourself. In the poem entitled **Have You Stopped To Think?**, the key points of self-perception are well illustrated.

Have you stopped to think why some men
are great
While other ones just remain small?
The big men feel big and they do big,
It's just how you feel, that's all.

If you feel success, you'll have success
Provided you also do, and
Follow your thoughts with the kind
of work
That's gonna' make it come true.

But you can't get big by feeling small
And you can only go as far
As your constant thoughts and your
daily deeds,
For just as you feel, you are.

So direct your thoughts and make
them fit
Whatever you'd like to see.
For as you feel, you are bound to live
And whatever you feel, you'll be.

The difference isn't always "I.Q." or special ability. The difference usually is determined by how people see themselves and how they feel about themselves. What they think they are capable of doing. As I related to you earlier in the first chapter, that's what Solomon meant when he said, "As a man thinketh in his heart, so is he." He's right too, for if you really feel something in your heart, your actions will follow through with that feeling.

Your present desires, ambitions, goals and future accomplishments are regulated by your present thinking. It really doesn't matter what your past thoughts have been . . . even if they were negative thoughts. What does matter is your present thought patterns of success and where you are going from here. You are what you think you are! So here is a crucial point . . . **YOU CAN CHANGE THE COURSE OF YOUR LIFE!** That's a staggering realization. You can move out of mediocrity and become a Mental Millionaire. You can increase your present capabilities. You can enjoy more success in life by increasing your self-concept and self-confidence. Sound exciting? Well, believe me, it is!

You are going to increase your success habits, your relationship with other people and, more importantly, your relationship with yourself. You are even going to find that you will have a deeper relationship with Almighty God. And when you do this, you'll find you take on a new lustre . . . a new courage for life itself. As St. Paul said, "Behold all things become new." It all depends upon your self-image . . . how you see yourself. You must begin by seeing yourself as being successful.

Dr. Maxwell Maltz, the famous plastic surgeon, author, lecturer and expert on self-image psychology, wrote, "A human being always acts and feels and performs in accordance with what he imagines to be true about himself and his environment." You simply can't get "big" by thinking small . . . you simply can't become a success if you see yourself as a failure, or even "average."

Most of your defeats do not come to you because someone possesses more ability than you possess. Those defeats generally come because you do not have the proper self-image along with the staying power to become successful. Many times other people are more successful than you simply because they have a better self-image of themselves. They see themselves as winners and, as a result, they are continually receiving the rewards, while you are getting, at best, honorable mention.

Read this poem very carefully, and then ask yourself this question: "Which person am I, according to my self-image?"

If you think you're beaten, you are.
If you think you dare not, you don't.
If you'd like to win but you think you can't,
Why it's almost certain you won't.

If you think you'll lose, you're lost.
For out in the world you find
Success begins with a fellow's will.
It's all in his state of mind.

If you think you're outclassed, you are.
You've got to think high to rise.
You've got to be sure of yourself
Before you can ever win a prize.

Now life's battles don't always go
To the stronger or faster man,
But sooner or later the man who wins
Is the man who thinks he can!

What kind of person do you really want to be? Are you that kind of person now? Is your total life spectrum a meaningful one? What do you dream of in the inner recesses of your mind? What is that one goal you would give almost anything in the world to achieve? And, most importantly, what are you doing about making your dreams come true? Do you see yourself as being able to accomplish those dreams? What is the self-image? Self is the identity character, or essential quality, that composes your personality as you see it within yourself. Image is the reflection you receive from the projection to others of your same self. Self-image, then, is the concept you have of yourself projected to others, their interpretation of yourself reflected back to you, and the impression you get from the reflection of the way in which they see you.

Each person sees himself as being a unique kind of individual. You have a combination of genes, traits, habits and characteristic patterns of behavior. You possess certain abilities, skills and knowledge. You hold various beliefs, values, and attitudes. You are being directed toward certain goals, aims and aspirations. You perceive yourself in relationship to the way you are relating to your surroundings; what objects you possess, what social groups you belong to, what your social status and roles are, how you are regarded in the eyes of other people. All these things together make up your total self-concept.

One of your major keys to life then is in developing the proper self-concept, or self-image that will reflect back to you a picture of yourself being successful. That's how you are going to become a Mental Millionaire. It doesn't just happen. You have to study, work and prepare yourself for success.

Abraham Lincoln said, "I'll study and get ready and then maybe my chance will come." He did study. He did prepare. And his chance did come! The fact is, our chances almost always come when we have studied and prepared ourselves. It takes study and preparation for us to even recognize chance or opportunity. We have chances and opportunities almost every day of our lives. But we often fail to recognize them--because of our lack of preparation.

As Confucius once said, "In all things, success depends upon previous preparation. Without such preparation there is sure to be failure." Preparation always starts with the important thing we call "attitude". And our attitudes are directly in proportion to our self-concepts, or self-images. Perception is the key to all of our lives, and we all perceive differently--Some positively, some negatively. That's why some people are successful and others are unsuccessful!

If you want to develop that type of possibility thinking which produces Mental Millionaires, you're going to have to understand that it's going to be based on understanding, faith, and action. As James said in the New Testament,

"Faith without works is dead." We become what we think about, and what we think about becomes our actions to behavior. If you have studied human behavior very carefully, you have learned that the process of individual growth and development is based on four progressive steps:

1. You are what you concentrate on.
2. What you concentrate on seems real.
3. What you concentrate on grows.
4. You always find what you concentrate on.

Therefore, a fundamental foundation for our perceptual life is based on understanding, faith, and action. The joke is told about the church that was voting on purchasing a chandelier. One old man was very opposed to purchasing a new chandelier and when he was confronted and asked why, he said, "Well, there are three reasons. Number one, no one knows how to spell it; Number two, no one knows how to play it; and Number three, what we really need is more light." Too many individuals are like that old man. We are opposed to change simply because we do not understand. We may have faith and we may produce action, but if we are traveling down the wrong road because we did not consult the map, our faith and actions are only working against us because we lack understanding.

Unfortunately, many people have a self-image of failure. They simply believe they cannot be successful. As a result of thinking about failure and concentrating upon it, their self-concept of failure grows, and they end up failing. They fail to achieve the goal and objective of being successful and developing the right mental attitudes because they simply don't perceive it as being possible . . . at least not for them.

Some people have a tendency to lock in on the overall self-concepts and miss the details that are so deeply involved in our perceptual world. Those small details could make all the difference between having a successful self-image and a failure self-image. By the same token, you have to be extremely careful that you do not magnify the details and ignore the larger picture. For example, you may do ten things right and one thing wrong. As a result of magnifying the details, you could have a tendency to ignore the ten things you did correctly and emphasize the one thing that was done incorrectly, thus creating a failure self-image. When this happens, people may have a tendency to see themselves as their mistakes, rather than seeing their mistakes simply as a part of them. Mistakes are to be experienced, learned from, and forgotten. Therefore, you must maintain a proper balance between the "big" picture and the "detail" picture of the self-image.

You are not your mistakes! They are only a part of you. Don't worry about making a mistake. Chances are very great that if you don't make mistakes, you're not doing anything. Right now you might be one of those individuals in the world who is selling yourself short on your real ability simply because you do not perceive yourself as being successful, or as being a winner. In reality, there is no limitation to your abilities. The only real competition is within you. Competition means pressure and pressure causes mistakes. You must begin by seeing yourself as a winner. Plant that winner image firmly in your mind. Burn it as deeply in the grooves of your mind as if you were engraving it upon wood.

Dr. Maxwell Maltz said, "You are not superior, you are not inferior, you are you!" There are people in this world who can perform some tasks better than you. There are other people who will be inferior to you in certain aspects of their performance. But the key is not whether you are superior or inferior to another person in any given task; the key is to be able to see yourself as you really are and what you are capable of becoming. Decide what your real talents are . . . then enter into competition with yourself to utilize those talents to the fullest extent. Develop your perceptual self-image to the point where you can maximize your potential.

When you give a speech, don't compare yourself to other public speakers. The important thing for you to realize is the fact that there are speakers who probably do a better job giving a speech than you do on certain occasions. There are probably certain occasions when you will do better than other speakers. But the key to the whole thing is this . . . Did you give 100% of what you had while you were making that speech? The point is you must give 100% of all your talents every time you perform a task.

You may give a speech and, let's say, there are 100 people present and 98 of them come by and tell you that you did a great job. Two out of the 100 may tell you that they weren't greatly impressed. Unfortunately, you may permit the 2% to take away all the joy that the 98% have shared with you. Why? Because you may have a tendency in your self-image to identify with the 2% that said your speech was poorly prepared instead of identifying with the 98% who said you were a success.

But even more important than whether someone else said your speech was a failure or success is your own perception of how well you did. Did you give 100% of your talent? If you gave 100% of your talent, then you can understand the fact that some people will be satisfied with your performance and some people will be dissatisfied. After all, if you've given 100% of all the talents you possess, you can't do any better at that moment regardless of how hard you try. So the fact that it didn't please someone doesn't bother you because that was one of your expectations. The fact that you gave 100% and it did please some, becomes a part of the reward you receive for a job well done.

H. W. Beecher said, "It is not what a man gets, but what a man IS that he should be concerned about. He should think first of his character and then of his condition. If he has the former, he need have no fears about the latter. Character will draw condition after it. Circumstances obey these principles."

Let's create a pragmatic situation and try to

illustrate for you how you sometimes miss some valuable keys to living because you often overlook pertinent details in your perceptual world. Below is a triangle, and inside that triangle is a sentence. Take just a second and read the sentence inside the triangle, then continue reading the chapter. We'll come back to the sentence inside the triangle a little later in the chapter.

As long as we're concentrating on perceptual details, I want you to participate in another project. By utilizing only the perceptual powers of the mind (without using your pencil or finger), mentally count the number of F's in the following sentence:

"Federal fuses are the result of years of scientific study combined with the experience of years."

Now you have participated in two perceptual projects. You read a sentence and you counted F's. Let's go back and look very carefully at those two projects. If you perceived like 98% of the American people, you probably made a couple of errors. The chances are you probably said that the sentence says, "Once in a lifetime." But if you'll go back and look very carefully, you will discover that the sentence reads, "Once in a a lifetime." There are two A's.

Now, take a look at the second project--counting the F's in the sentence. The chances are probably great you counted somewhere between two and six F's. How many F's are there? There are six. There is one each in "federal", "fuses", "scientific", and there are three "of's", making a total of six F's in the sentence.

If you happened to get incorrect answers the first time through the projects, your mental response to this will probably be somewhat defensive. You may have a tendency to give excuses, or try to justify your wrong answers. But the truth of the matter is that if you missed one of the A's in the sentence inside the triangle, or if you missed several of the F's, you did so because you misperceived some very pertinent details. One secret in becoming a Mental Millionaire is your ability to decipher those details that are extremely important to you in life. Details are often the difference between being right and being wrong. Between being successful and being unsuccessful.

Chances are very great that your husband, or your wife, or your child understands your overall philosophies of life very clearly. But where you get into the majority of your problems are with the details. For example, your children understand your philosophies of religion and your moral values. But what causes them a problem is when you park where it says "No Parking." A small detail? Yes. But that small detail can have a lasting effect on the lives of those individuals around you whom you are influencing. The speed limit is 55 miles an hour and you drive at 65 miles an hour. Small detail? Yes. But it is a detail of lasting importance in terms of the perceptual value of others whom you are influencing.

There are many small details which are key principles in life that you and I have a tendency to overlook. And while we often believe we are right in our perception--as in the sentence with the two A's or counting the F's--the reality of the situation is that the details which we often miss can make the difference between being successful and being unsuccessful . . . between being right and being wrong.

Let's try another project. I am going to ask you some questions, and you answer out loud as you read. How much are two and two? How much are four and four? How much are eight and eight? How much are sixteen and sixteen? Chances are excellent that you gave yourself the correct answers. Why? Basically, you gave yourself the correct answers because you have learned a system. That system we call "mathematics" and "addition", and you have learned it works well for you. We'll discuss Systems and their Importance in the next chapter.

Let's look at the problems listed below. In this system of addition we are interested in results. Here are twelve problems, all equaling fifty. Look them over very carefully.

27	19	46	38
+23	+31	+ 4	+11
50	50	50	50
14	21	33	42
+36	+29	+17	+ 8
50	50	50	50
15	28	40	32
+35	+22	+10	+18
50	50	50	50

Chances are very good that you disovered the mistake. 38 and 11 do not equal 50. Isn't it interesting that you were asked to read a sentence, and to count F's, and the chances of you getting incorrect answers were probably very good. But when I put something on a page that has one mistake on it, you find it immediately. What does this mean to you perceptually?

First of all, it means that what you perceived to be accurate may not have been accurately perceived, as you witnessed in the first two examples. Secondly, you discovered that it's much easier to see the mistakes of others than it is to see your own. Therefore, psychologically, you may have a tendency to ignore those areas in your life that can be developed and, in most cases, developed rather easily, and simply write them off as human nature or endeavor to give excuses to cover up the imperfections.

Understanding yourself . . . what makes you tick . . . and understanding your self-perception isn't an easy matter, even after reading many books and studying for hours and hours. You will be tempted to perceive the world the way your particular needs and mechanisms combine to make you see it--to give life special meaning for you. If you are consistently unable to do this, your personality cannot keep in balance and the result will be chaos. Once you have adopted a particular perceptual view of the world as a result of your own needs, you will be reluctant to change, or give up, that view or to see other aspects of the world which may not be as comfortable for you or as consistent with your attitudes and values. Then you can either distort what you see in line with your needs, or you can refuse to see it altogether.

To illustrate how difficult it is for us to see things another way once we have become set in our attitudes, or in our particular perceptual view of a situation, let's look at the following picture.

Young woman or old woman? Which do you see?
(From W. E. Hill)

Taking A Look At Yourself

What do you see? A young woman? That's right. There is her hat with its flowing scarf and her heavy coat around her shoulders. Her head is turned to the right so that only the tip of her nose is in profile. All of her clothes date back to the early 1900's. Just a minute, though. Someone else says that it is not a young woman at all . . . it's an old woman. There is her scarf over her head. There is her long nose. She looks like a wrinkled peasant. Actually, both are right. There is a young woman in the picture and there is an old woman in it. The interesting thing about this picture is that once you see the young woman, it takes a long time to see the old woman, and vice-versa. Even in a simple little matter like this, it is very difficult to change one's attitudes. People can sit for hours and look at this picture, seeing only one part of it but not the other. And people can sit for hours and argue with each other without seeing the other side of the argument.

Thus, we learn another lesson about perception. We have learned that you and I have a tendency to fixate--to lock in on certain ideas, attitudes, and values. Some people may never be able to really adjust or perform the systems defined throughout this book because they are so used to perceiving the world through their eyes that a new experience, a new insight, a new hope, becomes almost a complete impossibility to them. Why? Simply because they have "locked into" one way of thinking and are unable to expand the exposure of their mind. They have fixated. It's the Young woman OR the Old woman, but never the possibility of both women in one picture.

The way we personally perceive the world is extremely important to our total self-development. But the way we perceive ourselves and establish our self-images and self-concepts is even more important. How successful can you be? That question can only be answered with another question . . . How successful do you want to be?

There's nothing too good for you
to possess
Nor heights you cannot real.
Your power is more than your
thoughts or guess,
It's something you have to feel.

There's nothing to fear
Your innerself knows
That you're the infinite you.
So set your heart on the highest
mount
There's nothing you cannot do.

You've got to believe that. You've got to create a self-image that says, "While I'm not perfect, I do a lot of things right. While I make some mistakes, I'm not my mistakes." The Bible teaches you that you have been created in the image of Almighty God. That you are a worthy individual. Worthy of all the riches this world has to offer you--spiritually, financially, mentally, socially and physically. It tells us in

First Peter, chapter 2, verse 9, that we are a chosen generation, a royal priesthood, a holy nation, a peculiar people. I guarantee that if you apply the principles of becoming a Mental Millionaire, you'll be peculiar because you'll be part of that two percent who gets more living out of life and more life out of living.

So, create in your mind a positive self-image. You can become whatever you can perceive. I remember learning a phrase as a young boy which I have never forgotten. "What the mind of man can perceive, man can achieve." How true that is, if you'll simply believe.

Since I believe very strongly that thoughts only become real when they are placed into action, listed below are eight attitudes that I feel will help you cultivate your positive self-image. See yourself as being:

1. Cheerful.
2. Tolerant.
3. Truthful.
4. Understanding.
5. Tactful.
6. Thankful.
7. Adaptable.
8. Confident.

Don't try to do all of these in one day or even in one week. But do one each week, and then in just eight short weeks, you will have accomplished the attitudes of each characteristic.

As we talk about your self-image, let me throw out a challenge to you. When you are

tempted to feel that you can't accomplish anything; when you are tempted to feel that you
don't have time to practice the principles related
in this book; re-read this portion of the book
again and consider the accomplishments of an
early day Virginian. Before he died in 1826, this
man had:

* Finished college in less than
  three years.

* Studied law and been admitted
  to the bar at the age of 24.

* Introduced crop rotation and
  terracing to the United States.

* Designed and built his own home,
  designed one of the nation's leading
  universities, and designed the
  Capitol Building of his state.

* Invented a plow, a manifold signing
  machine, letter copy press, double
  swinging doors, a seven day calendar
  clock and countless gadgets.

* Originated the decimal system for
  United States currency.

* Played the violin well.

* Become a serious student of
  natural history, Indian languages,

Latin, Greek, Italian, French,
German, Anglo-Saxon, mathematics, history, geography, civics,
economics and philosophy.

* Served as a member of his State
  Legislature, Governor of his State,
  Minister to France, Secretary of
  State, Vice President and President
  of the United States for two terms.

* Created the public school system
  in his State.

* Become President of a University.

* Established the U.S. Military
  Academy and designed the uniforms
  the cadets still wear today.

* Written the rules of Parliamentary
  Procedure under which the United
  States Senate still operates.

* Was an excellent host . . . enjoyed
  entertaining.

* Fought for a system of govern-
  ment that made the United States
  a democratic republic, not one
  ruled by the aristocracy.

* Wrote over 16,000 letters to friends
  and colleagues all over the world.

    *   Designed his own gravestone
and created the epitaph listing
the three accomplishments of
which he was the proudest:
"Here was buried Thomas
Jefferson, Author of the Dec-
laration of Independence, of
the Statutes of Virginia for
Religious Freedom, and Father
of the University of Virginia."

Thomas Jefferson's endless list of accomplishments offers much for all Americans to
admire. He had tremendous efficiency for
use of time, an excellent example for all of us
to seek to emulate. He had a beautiful self-
image. But alas, many of us still have a tendency to get bogged down, wringing our hands
and lamenting, "I just can't do it. It's just not
in me. I just don't have enough time." Next
time you begin experiencing those feelings,
turn back and read this section of the book
again that illustrates the accomplishments of
Thomas Jefferson, and then remember that your
self-image today will determine your accomplishments for tomorrow.

You're not going to achieve that self-image
overnight. It requires work . . . hard work.
Adequate preparation helps you recognize the
potential riches around you. Whatever you are
going to be tomorrow, you are becoming today.

On his deathbed, a Chasidic Rabbi once made
this statement, "When I was young I set out to
change the world. When I grew a little older,

I perceived that this was too ambitious so I set out to change my State. This too I realized as I grew older, was too ambitious, so I set out to change my town. When I realized I could not do even that, I tried to change my family. Now, as an old man, I know I should have started by changing myself. If I had started with myself, then maybe I would have succeeded in changing my family, the town, or even the State . . . and who knows? Maybe even the world!!!"

Stand in front of the mirror. Take a good look at yourself. You are viewing an individual who is worthy of all the successes that God has made available to us in this world. You need only to understand, believe, have faith and receive. The Bible tells us that we have not because we ask not. So I want you to ask for the very best. Have faith and believe that it will come. But in so doing, always remember the words of James in the New Testament: "Faith without works is dead!"

CHAPTER 3

THE THREE KEYS TO SUCCESS

"In the beginning God created the heaven and the earth. So God created Man in His own image, in the image of God created He Him; male and female created He them."
Genesis 1:1 and 27

In the last chapter you learned that you have a tremendous responsibility to develop the proper self-concept or self-image. You must believe in yourself to the extent that you know you can become successful. You must perceive yourself as an individual with a burning desire to achieve success and reach your personal goals.

We also shared eight attitudes which you need to cultivate in order to create the right self-image to assist you in becoming a Mental Millionaire.

Now, the question is this . . . How do I do it? How do I put it all together to make it work for me? You have read books on how to be successful. You have probably heard various motivational type speeches on how to achieve your goals and reach your full potential. But once you get away from that inspiring book or that motivating speech or that positive environment, you may have a tendency to forget what you have read, or heard, or experienced. Maybe you even try to make the ideas work for you, but they don't seem to hold up under the stress of time. So you developed an attitude that went something like this: "Well, maybe it works for other people, but I can't seem to get it to work for me.

I wish someone could really tell me how to make a success out of my life."

The answer to that question is so simple that mankind has overlooked it for centuries. Human beings have a tendency to complicate all aspects of living. Out of my past experiences as a high school teacher, an Associate Professor of Psychology, a Manager in the Industrial environment, a Consultant to the Business and Industrial world, and as a Minister of the Gospel, I have spent a great deal of time watching and observing those individuals, companies, hospitals, and churches who have been successful. I would analyze them very carefully, trying to discover the key characteristics, traits, and combinations that made them successful. What causes some individuals to have a good mental attitude while others appear to have been raised on sour grapes? What causes some people to develop the philosophy of becoming Mental Millionaires in their lives while others perceive life as a bore?

Through all that empirical observation, I discovered that some key elements were continually present in those people and institutions who were successful. In this chapter I'm going to share those keys with you. In the remainder of this book we will cover some vital keys to build into those elements in order to become a Mental Millionaire.

But before I do that, it's extremely important that I share with you what I call "The Three Keys To Success." Without these three keys, you will never be successful. Once you have established the fact that you have within you a burning desire to be successful, to have a better marriage, to create financial security, to become a Mental Millionaire and get more living out of life and more life out of living, you will need some type of road map to follow to reach your desired destination. For centuries people have tried to understand what makes other people successful. In many cases they even tried to imitate them, to copy them, or to become like them in some way. Unfortunately, that is not the answer. Therefore, what I'm about to share with you right now is one of the greatest secrets known to man today. Learn it, and learn it well . . . for your future depends upon your ability to apply it!

I was born in the State of Missouri, in the small town of Leadwood, which is located about 70 miles south of St Louis. The town basically survived because of the industry of the St. Joe Lead Mining Company. Out of that early experience I developed a philosophy like most Missourians, whereby in order for me to accept something, I must be shown. As you well know, Missouri has long been known as the "Show Me State." Therefore, as I looked for the answers to success, I looked at the different approaches and philosophies with a very jaundiced eye. I tried to analyze very carefully the characteristics which I perceived in order to separate the wheat from the chaff. But in each case where I found a successful individual, a successful company, a successful hospital, a successful business, a successful Mental Millionaire, I always found that at the basic core there were three keys to their success. I challenge you to try them for yourself. And once you have, you are going to discover that these three keys to success will literally change your life, your marriage, your financial condition, your daily living. And if you get nothing else out of this book, take what I am about to share with you as the keys to your future success.

As Consultants, Jim Cavanaugh and I are always placed on the line to produce. We are continually faced with one basic question . . . Does it work? Do the philosophies and the ideas and the suggestions and the solutions we render to our clients really work? That's what the client wants to know. And only when they work are we then financially rewarded for our input into the various consulting situations. Since we were continually put on the spot to perform, to produce positive results, we wanted to make certain that the keys to success which we had discovered were valid. Here is how we validated the concept of our three keys to success.

First of all, we went into many businesses, industries, and hospitals and had discussions with top management individuals to determine what had been adopted as their philosophy of management for their institutions. There were some who said, "Our philosophy of management is Management By Results. Results are the only things that really matter." We want to get production out the back door! We want our patients to be happy! They had developed a philosophy of saying, "We manage by results."

There were other managers who had accepted

a management philosophy of Management By Objectives. Basically, their philosophy was one of setting objectives and goals, and then following through to see that each employee did their part in achieving those goals and objectives.

There were still other managers who had adopted a philosophy of Management By Example. They believed that if the manager would set the right example, then the employees would follow that example and thus, results would be indicated in terms of a successful operation.

There were other managers who had identified with the philosophy of Mr. Joe Badden and believed the answer was in being Tough-Minded. You must be firm, but fair. Don't be like a piece of granite that will shatter when hit with a hammer, but rather, be like a piece of leather. The hammer may leave an indentation, but the original form is still strong and tough.

So we grouped the various companies who had identified their concept or philosophy of management as being Management By Results, put them in a list, and we analyzed very carefully their operations. What we found was very interesting, but not too surprising. We found that some of those institutions and businesses who were managing by results were very successful; not without their problems . . . (I like to call these "opportunities" and we will talk about problems and opportunities later on in the book) . . . but successful. We found that other institutions and businesses using the same philosophy were what we might call "average" in terms of performance, and we found others that were doing very poorly. Amazingly enough, as we went through each of the identified concepts of management--Management By Objectives, Management By Example, Tough-Minded Management, etc., we discovered the same answers in each given group of management styles. Some companies were being very successful while others were doing rather average or mediocre, and yet others were doing rather poorly in their performance for success. Very quickly, it was obvious to see that the answer to success then did not lie in one system of management. If that were the case, all of those operating within any one style or system of management would have been successful and would have given us an answer immediately. So we had empirical input, but we certainly did not have an answer to our question of what produces success.

We decided then to go beyond the realm of business, industry and hospitals, and look at the home environment for possible answers and insight to our question. We identified three basic parental styles or philosophies for raising children . . . those being basically the authoritarian, the democratic, and the permissive styles of raising children. The authoritarian parent's philosophy would go something like this . . . They say to the child, "I don't care what you think, as long as you put your feet under my table and live under my roof you're going to abide by my rules and regulations. When you get out on your own, then that's your business, you do what you want to do. But as long as you are here in this house, you are going to do what I tell you."

We surveyed a second group and classified them as being democratic in their philosophy of raising children. If a problem were to exist they would say to the child something like this . . . "Johnny, I realize we have a problem; that obviously your mother and I aren't communicating with you very well; that some hard feelings exist. I think we should sit down and openly discuss these problems and see if we can't work them out". The basic idea here being, let's be open, let's be honest, let's communicate with each other and see if we can't solve our problems in a democratic way.

The third basic group we surveyed was what we might call the permissive parents. These parents pretty much give the child a free rein of activities within the household. They might adopt a philosophy like this . . . If Johnny is sawing off one leg of the piano bench, he should saw off the other three to make it level. But whatever you do, don't discipline or thwart Johnny in any way because it might stymie his growth as an individual. Give him full freedom of expression.

An interesting observation in this situation is that we discovered basically the same results we discovered in the business, industrial and hospital environments . . . that there were some authoritarian parents whose children turned out be be extremely well adjusted. There were other children who had the natural day to day type problems, and there were other children who turned out to be juvenile deliquents. However, the same patterns of behavior remained true of the democratic parents as well as the permissive parents. So once again we discovered the answer was not in the style of raising children. Success and delinquency were found in all three styles. Therefore, it seemed obvious to us that the answer might well lie in looking at those businesses, industries, hospitals, and parents who had been successful. We needed to analyze them all very carefully to discover what common characteristics might exist within all those successful cases in order to find the Keys to Success. So analyze we did! And our discovery was so amazing and yet so simple . . . so simple that man has overlooked it for centuries.

As we shared with you in the very beginning of this Chapter, we could have read the 1st Chapter of Genesis and have learned our secret from the Holy Bible. Yet, while many of us are students of the Bible, we sometimes fail to correlate what the Bible is saying to our various projects in life, as I certainly did in this specific project.

It tells us in the Book of Genesis that God created the heavens and the earth. He created the universe in which we live. Now, regardless of our religious or philosophical discussions of how the universe came into existence, I think you will have to agree with me that the universe in which we live works extremely well. The Bible also relates to us in the 27th verse of the 1st Chapter of Genesis that He created male and female--the human body. I'm sure again that you will agree that the human body is a perfect piece of mechanism. It is a masterpiece! There are things about the human body that we do not understand even today with all our modern technology. Therefore, these two examples brought to light the first key we discovered about success from the research which we did. So, let's proceed and discover these Keys to Success.

The first Key to Success: YOU MUST HAVE A SYSTEM. The universe is a system. The human body is a system. The automobile you drive is a system. The computer that prints your payroll checks is a system. Stop and think of the things around you that work so well and you'll find they are systems. Your washer, dryer, trash compactor, hot water heater . . . and on and on and on!

In order to become a Mental Millionaire . . . to establish the proper positive mental attitudes that will cause you to get more living out of life and more life out of living . . . you must have a system. You must have "how-to" examples. You must have a road map to follow to your destination. In short, you must have a system! And the better that system is understood, the better will be your success.

For just a moment, pause and take a look at your life. If I were to ask you what your system is for raising children, I wonder if you could really tell me. You should be able to. You should be able to share with me your system of raising children. But could you really do it? What is the system under which your household operates? If you have small children, what does your system say about eating their dinner? Can they take all they want and leave part of it on their plates? If they put food on their plates, must they eat it all? If they eat what they take, are they then entitled to dessert? If they don't eat what they take, are they not entitled to dessert? Is there a system involved in raising your family or does it depend on how you feel at the moment? Does your system depend upon the system, or your attitude?

Take a look at another area. What is your system of managing money, or, as some people call it, budgeting? Have you established a system for the distribution of your finances? Or do you simply receive the paycheck and pay and distribute until it runs out and then somebody has to wait? Have you established a system of financing that says pay yourself first? Do you always put 10% of what you make away? Does your system say pay other people first, and if there's anything left, I'll take some then? Or does your system say the first 10% goes to the church? The point is this . . . you MUST have a system. What is your system for living?

Maybe you're not happy. You don't think you can find happiness in life. What you need is a system for finding happiness in your life. Take time to write out your system of operation. I recommend that you pause right now, take one area of your life . . . whatever area you may choose . . . and start making a list of what you perceive your system should be in that area. Chances are great you're going to discover that it's extremely difficult to put down specifics on paper. Why? Because you have been doing something for a number of years in a vague, abstract way without a system. Each one of you, by the time you have finished this book, should be able to define for your husband, your wife, or whomever, your system of living. You should be able to define your system for raising your children. You should be able to define your system for budgeting the dollars that come into your house. Whatever the area may be, if you plan to be successful, you must have a system. You must have a road map to follow. No one else can create that system for you. YOU must do it. You are a unique individual and you must design that system to meet your individual needs and wants. You are going to discover that once you have put together your system, you will be surprised at how much more quickly you will achieve success and accomplish your daily goals.

Before you move on to the next point, let me make one thing clear. You have learned that any system will work . . . management by results, management by objectives, raising your children the authoritarian way, or raising your children by permissive means . . . any system will work if you will work the system. The better the system is defined, written out and understood, the greater will be your chances for success. Thus the first Key to Success is to have a well-defined, workable system.

This leads us to the second point in our three Keys to Success. Going back to our two original examples of the universe and the human body, which we agreed work extremely well, we discover our second Key to Success. Looking at the universe, let's take the sun . . . it always comes up in the east and it always sets in the west. It doesn't sometimes decide to come up in the west and set in the east. If it did, a lot of us would be extremely upset.

Let's look at the second example, the human body. The blood that flows through the human heart goes in the atrium and out the ventricle. In the top and out the bottom. It does this time and time and time again. But if suddenly the blood should decide to go from the bottom to the top, you have a serious problem.

Let's take a look at a third example . . . your automobile. Like the universe and the human body, it is also a system. We have Fords, Chryslers, and Chevrolets. We have front wheel drives, rear wheel drives, and we have four wheel drives. We have all kinds of systems. They're all different but they all work. The automobile has within it something that is just as vital to its function as the heart is to the human body or the rising and setting of the sun is to the universe, and that something gives us our second Key to Success . . . consistency. The sun always comes up in the east and always sets in the west. The blood always goes in to the atrium and comes out the ventricle. You turn on the key to the ignition and the car can be started. That is a Key to Success . . . consistency.

Many managers talk about morale problems. They say, "I can't understand where I have gone wrong." What types of managers have morale problems? Authoritarian managers? Democratic managers? Permissive managers? They all have morale problems from time to time. But there is one kind of manager that usually has more morale problems and that is the inconsistent manager. This manager may come in every day with a sour expression, and then one day he comes in smiling. That is going to create questions in the minds of his employees.

The next time you want to start your automobile, you expect that engine to turn over. You expect that performance consistently. And if the engine doesn't start, you get upset. Yet we seem to be amazed that people get upset with us when we become inconsistent. What would happen if you purchased an item in New York City for seventy-five cents, you gave them a dollar, and they gave you fifteen cents change? Your comment would probably be, "Hey, you short-changed me." Why? Because in giving you your change, that clerk became inconsistent with the system that we have accepted in the United States of America. Seventy-five cents subtracted from one dollar will always give you twenty-five cents change . . . forgetting taxes.

Many times parents will come to us and say, "Where did I go wrong? I taught my child the Bible, I taught him the elements of Christianity, I taught him moral codes, and yet I end up with a juvenile delinquent. What went wrong?" Let me share a secret with you. One of the things we've discovered is that juvenile delinquents don't come from rich homes or poor homes or authoritarian homes or democratic homes. They come from inconsistent homes. Just like morale problems come from inconsistent managers.

Let me give you an example of how this concept of inconsistency works so that you may be more aware of the importance of consistency. Because the moment we become inconsistent, our system, regardless of how well it has been defined and established, begins to break down. Let's assume for a moment that you are working at a job as an executive in some operation and it's merit review time. Hopefully, you are going to get a good evaluation and receive a raise. You have your meeting that day with your boss and you discuss your performance very thoroughly. You go home that night and as you walk in the door your spouse says, "Honey, did you get the raise?" You say, "Well, he wants to think about it for another day." So at this point in time you're not feeling too well . . . you feel a little insecure. You're questioning whether or not you're going to get that raise you need so badly. You're questioning why he wanted to think about it another day. Therefore, your attitude just isn't up to par. So you sit down to eat and one of your children eats a couple of bites and says to you, "Daddy, I'm full. I'm going to go play." What do you say? "No, you're not! You're not going out to play. You're going to sit there and eat everything on your plate! I'm working hard to earn money to put food on the table. There are children in the world starving to death. Etc., etc., etc. Now eat!"

The next day you to to work and sure enough,

you get the raise. You come home that night and you're very happy, very jubilant. You have an excellent positive attitude. You go through the same process. You sit down to eat. Your child eats a couple of bites and says she's full and wants to go play. What do you say? You may respond like this . . . "That's alright, honey. Run along. Go ahead. Have a good time." But your system now is inconsistent. You have permitted your feelings and attitudes to destroy the system, if you had one in the first place. One time you tell her she can't go out and play after eating a couple of bites, and yet another time you tell her she can go play after eating just a couple of bites. She has no system to which she can relate. She doesn't know what is right or wrong within your given family structure. A system has become inconsistent. That's what produces juvenile delinquency . . . inconsistency. Even though your philosophy of religion and your major philosophies of how the house should be run, and your moral code of ethics are understood, it is most important that in order to be successful, you do not place inconsistencies into the system.

Have you ever been in the hospital? We have many fine hospitals, all working very hard to provide good patient care. But let me share another secret with you. Those hospitals are filled with patients for simply one reason . . . because that system of the human body has become inconsistent. That inconsistency may be a heart attack, a gall bladder attack, an appendicitis attack, or cancer. But one thing is certain . . . there is an inconsistency in the system. The patient will leave the hospital when either he has terminated or his system has been brought back into consistency . . . or what we call, returned to normal.

Let me reiterate these two points. First of all, you must have a system. Secondly, that system must be consistent if you expect to see success. This leads to the third key necessary to produce success.

Take a pencil in your hand, stretch your arm out forward, let loose of the pencil and see what happens to it. It fell, didn't it? If you were to do that a hundred times, that pencil would fall a hundred times. Why does the pencil fall? Because the system of this universe, which is so consistent, has an element of control called gravity. Throw a ball in the air and it will come back down to the earth. Put an airplane in the air and cut all power and it will come to the ground. All because the elements of the universe are controlled by gravity.

Our second example of the human body also has an element of control. Let's assume this morning you woke up with beads of perspiration on your forehead. You don't have too many blankets on the bed and the room is not too hot. What's the problem? It doesn't take you long to discover you have a fever. An element in the human body . . . a thermostat, so to speak . . . is relating to you that you have a problem. Your body is sending you a message that something in your system is becoming inconsistent and starting to get out of control. It's time to do something about it. Take care of it. Make that inconsistency become consistent and bring it back under control.

Anything in the world that works will always have the three Keys to Success that we have discussed in this chapter. A system . . . consistency . . . and control. Look at our manufacturing operations. We have a product that is built through a system and we build it consistently day in and day out. But we have people stationed along the way at quality control checkpoints to make sure that our system is being consistent so the final product will always be the same. Remember, anything in the world that works has these three elements. There is no doubt the system will work for you if you will consistently work and control the system.

With these ideas in mind, let me share with you a system which I call twelve steps to good personal adjustment. I asked you earlier in the Chapter to write out several systems. To assist you with that project, I will discuss **A** system . . . not **the** system . . . but **a** system that will help you get better personal adjustment out of your life. In order to do this, let me begin by asking you some questions.

Do minor problems and disappointments throw you into a dither? Do you find it difficult to get along with people and are people having trouble getting along with you? Do the small pleasures of life fail to satisfy you? Are you unable to stop thinking about your anxieties? Do you fear people or situations that never used to trouble you? Are you suspicious of people . . .

mistrust your friends? Do you become frustrated because other people don't measure up to your standards? Do you feel inadequate and suffer the tortures of self-doubt? If your answer is "Yes" to most of these questions, there are some simple, practical, constructive things you can do. There is a system you can establish that will assist you to overcome these problems. But remember, success will not come from a half-hearted effort . . . nor will it come overnight. It's going to take some determination, some persistence, and some time. The results will certainly be worth your best efforts, whether it be an occasional mild upset which most of us experience or a problem that is more lasting and severe.

Let's look now at the twelve steps to good personal adjustment . . . a system to assist you in becoming a Mental Millionaire!

Step 1. **TALK IT OUT.** When something worries you, talk it out. Don't bottle it up. Confide your worries to some level-headed individual you can trust . . . your superior, an associate, your clergyman, whomever. Talking things out helps relieve the strain, reduces anxiety and helps you to see your worry in a clearer light and to recognize a solution.

Step 2. **ESCAPE FOR AWHILE.** Sometimes when things go wrong, it helps to escape for awhile. Making yourself stand there and suffer is a form of self-punishment, not a way to solve a problem. It is perfectly realistic and healthy to escape an emotional situation long enough to recover your breath and your balance. But be prepared to come back and deal with your difficulty when you are more composed, and when you and others involved are in better condition, both intellectually and emotionally.

Step 3. **WORK OFF YOUR ANGER.** If you feel yourself using anger as a general way of behavior, remember that while anger may give you a temporary sense of righteousness or even power, it will generally leave you feeling foolish and sorry in the end. If you feel like lashing out at someone who has provoked you, try holding off that impulse for awhile. Let it wait until tomorrow. Meanwhile, do something constructive with the pent-up energy. Working the anger out of your system and cooling off will leave you much better prepared to handle your problems intelligently and gainfully.

Step 4. **GIVE IN OCCASIONALLY.** If you find yourself getting into frequent quarrels with people and feeling obstinate and defiant, remember that's the behavior of a frustrated child. Stand your ground on what you know is right . . . but do so calmly and make allowances for the fact that you could turn out to be wrong. Remember the "Once In A Lifetime" or the counting of the F's in Chapter 2. And even if you are dead right . . . it's easier on your system to give in once in awhile.

Step 5. **DO SOMETHING FOR OTHERS.** If you feel yourself worrying all the time, try doing something for someone else. You'll find this will take the sting out of your own worries, and even better yet, give you a feeling of having been of service to others.

Step 6. **TAKE ONE THING AT A TIME.** For people under tension, an ordinary workload can sometimes seem unbearable. The load looks so great that it becomes painful to tackle any part of it, even the things that most need to be done. When that happens, remember that it is a temporary condition and that you can work your way out of it. The surest way to do this is take a few of the most urgent tasks and pitch into them. One at a time. Set aside all the rest for the time being. Once you dispose of these, you'll see that the remainder is not such a horrible task after all. You'll be in the swing of things and the rest of the tasks will go much more easily.

Step 7. **SHUN THE SUPERMAN URGE.** Some people expect too much from themselves and get into a constant state of worry and anxiety because they think they are not achieving as much as they should. They try for perfection in almost everything. Admirable as this ideal is, it is an open invitation to failure. No one can be perfect in everything. Remember, **you are not your mistakes; they're simply a part of you.**

Step 8. **GO EASY WITH YOUR CRITICISM.** Some people expect too much of others and then feel frustrated, let down, or disappointed when another person does not measure up to their standards. The other person may be an employee, or co-member of management, or a member of your family whom you are trying to fit into a preconceived pattern . . . perhaps even trying to change to suit yourself. Remember, each person has his own virtues, his own shortcomings, his own values and his own right to develop as an individual. People who feel let down by the shortcomings (real or imagined) of others are really let down by themselves. Instead of being too critical about the other person's behavior, search out the good points and help him develop those points to the fullest extent.

Step 9. GIVE THE OTHER FELLOW A BREAK. When people are under emotional tension they often feel they have to get there first. . to edge out the other person. . even if the goal is as trivial as getting ahead on the highway. It need not be this way. Competition is contagious, but so is cooperation. When you give the other fellow a break, you very often make things easier for yourself. If he no longer feels you are a threat to him, he stops being a threat to you.

Step 10. MAKE YOURSELF AVAILABLE. Many of you have the feeling you are being left out, slighted, neglected, or rejected. Often you just imagine that other people feel this way about you when in reality they are eager for you to make the first move. Maybe you, not the others, are the one who is depreciating yourself. Instead of shrinking away and withdrawing, it is much healthier as well as more practical to continue to make yourself available. . . to make some of the overtones instead of always waiting to be asked. Of course, the opposite of withdrawal is equally futile. . pushing yourself forward on every occasion. This is often misinterpreted and may lead to real rejection. There's a middle ground between withdrawal and pushing. Try it. . it works!

Step 11. SCHEDULE YOUR RECREATION. Many people drive themselves so hard they allow themselves too little time for the recreation essential for good physical and mental health. They find it hard to make themselves take time out. For such people, a set routine and schedule will help. . . a program of definite hours when they will engage in some type of recreation. In general, it is desirable for almost everyone to have a hobby that absorbs them in off hours. One into which they can throw themselves completely and with pleasure. . . forgetting all about their daily work.

Step 12. SPEND TIME IN PRAYER AND MEDITATION. You and I have a decision to make as we live our lives. That decision may well be medication or meditation. There are many things in life that we perceive to be impossible. Yet if some way, some how, through our prayer and meditation we can come to the realization, as did St. Paul, that we can do all things through Christ which strengtheneth us, we will find that we have a member on our team that is invaluable. Set up a daily schedule, whether it's early in the morning or late at night, and take the time and the opportunity to communicate with Almighty God. Someone once said that prayer is man talking to God. . and Bible reading is God talking to man. Spend time in prayer so that you may talk with God, but also spend time reading and meditating in order that God, through the Bible, may talk with you.

There. . you have a system! Twelve sound steps that will assist you in good personal adjustment. It is a system that will work for you if you will work for it. You may want to add to this list, or you may want to adjust it to fit your personal needs. . . whatever it takes to make the system successful for you. The point is, you MUST develop a system for living.

If you develop a system for becoming a Mental Millionaire, and you are not consistent, and you do not work at controlling the system, the system will not work regardless of how good it was in its conception. You must dedicate yourself to taking the tools available to you and establishing the system and then being consistent with it.

> Isn't it strange that princes and kings
> And clowns that caper in sawdust rings
> And common people like you and me
> Are builders of eternity?
>
> Each is given a bag of tools,
> A shapeless mass and a book of rules,
> And each of us make 'ere life has flown
> A stumbling block or a stepping stone.

That stepping stone in our lives is a system that's consistent and well-controlled. If you don't utilize these Three Keys to Success in your system, then you're going to find stumbling block after stumbling block causing you to fall and fail. It's not because you're not able to rise above it. . it's because you haven't applied the self-discipline of consistency and control to the system which you have selected to live by.

CHAPTER 4

LEARN HOW TO LIVE WITH YOURSELF

By now you have some idea of how your self-image develops and all the different, complex situations that go into making you what you are. Every minute of your waking hours your self-image reacts as a protective agent to the world around you. The plant or the office in which you work, the people you work with, your wife or husband, your children, your neighbors and all the big and little events of the day, all go into making up your self-perception. What your personality, or self-image, or you, per se, would like to do, and what your environment and the world you live in allows you to do, are oftentimes quite different. This will create conflicts for you. (Conflicts will be discussed in Chapter 7). Your environment may make demands on you that your self-image can't or doesn't want to meet. You may be holding down a job that's too difficult for you, or working with or for someone you don't like. You may be carrying responsibilities that you're having a tendency to resent. But most of the time, your personality, or your self-concept, is pretty much in tune with your environment.

Actually there's a kind of give-and-take between the two. In part we have a tendency to react to our environment. On the other hand, if we develop a philosophy of acting, rather than reacting, we are in a situation to change some parts of our environment to suit the demands of our self-image. In fact, your self-image keeps trying to find ways to achieve harmony with your environment, while meeting your individual needs.

As a result of this continual adjustment process going on, we have in many cases developed what we call "defense mechanisms" to protect our self-image when we get into situations that either are uncomfortable or which we don't feel we know how to control. Basically we will either withdraw from the situation, clam up, become quiet, refuse to participate, or we will become aggressive. We may get loud, we may argue, we may show a lot of hostility, but we let it be known that we have a conflict between our present self-image and our environmental surroundings.

The third way of adjusting to the situation is what we call compromise. We may give and take in certain situations. If, for example, our self-image would like to accomplish one goal and we find it impossible or impractical to achieve that goal, we then will compromise and achieve another goal, often in an entirely different area. Let me illustrate this point by using the example of a young boy who would like to play on the high school football team but does not have the physical size or stamina to participate. He, therefore, might compromise and become the equipment manager of the team, or he might decide to excell in academic courses to counterbalance his inability to make the football team.

But in most of those situations we are not able to adjust to or control, we have a tendency to be more defensive and protect our self-images. The understanding of this concept is extremely important if you are going to become a Mental Millionaire.

The odds are that your biggest problems in life do not lie with your husband, or your wife, or your mother, or your father, or your boss, or your peers at work. Your biggest problems in life lie within yourself. If something doesn't go right, many times your defense mechanism will become aggressive and you may have a tendency to blame others. That all started back in the Garden of Eden. Adam blamed Eve, and Eve blamed the serpent for the problem that existed. But, the problem back in the Garden of Eden wasn't the apple on the tree. . . it was the "pair" on the ground.

You may often reach out and blame others when in reality, if you would look very carefully, you would find that the source of success or failure comes back to you. . not someone else. I recall hearing a speaker make an illustration that I have never forgotten. He said, "Every time you point a finger at someone else, there are three fingers pointing back at you."

The result of a majority of the incidents that occur to you in your lifetime are in direct proportion to your attidude. . whether you have reacted or whether you have acted. There are millions of people in America today who simply have not learned the art of how to live with themselves.

Learn To Live With Yourself

A woman said to me once, "Wherever I go, I have to take myself along, and that kind of spoils it all." Isn't it sad that this woman has not learned the art of living with herself? She searched everywhere to find happiness, but regardless of how hard she tried, it couldn't be found because it did not exist within her. Happiness must come from within you.

The joke has often been made that in search of happiness, we take vacations to Florida, or California, or "Lost Wages," Nevada. But the truth of the matter is that unless that happiness comes from within us. . unless we can take it along and share it. . unless we have learned the art of living with ourselves. . we're probably never going to find happiness somewhere else. People spend a lifetime trying to find security. But let me share another secret with you. Security cannot be found in your job, or in your home, or in the dollars you have in the bank. The only place security can really exist is within you. The secret is knowing that your security, which you feel within yourself, is your greatest asset. Within YOU. YOUR asset. Not from outside. Not from someone else. But YOU are the key. If you can grasp hold of the idea that you and God are a majority, and that together all things are possible, you can create a new meaning for your life. We learn to live with ourselves when we develop the right attitudes about ourselves and about others.

In the first chapter we discussed what you think of yourself. We tell a great deal about what we think of ourselves and how we have learned

to live with ourselves, by the company we keep.
Veronica Denal wrote this poem entitled, **You
Tell On Yourself.**

You tell on yourself by the friends you seek,
By the very manner in which you speak,
By the way you employ your leisure time.
By the use you make of a dollar or dime.

You tell what you are by the clothes you
wear,
By the spirit in which your burdens you
bear,
By the kind of things at which you laugh,
By the records you play on your phono-
graph.

You tell what you are by the way you walk,
By the things of which you delight to talk,
By the manner in which you bear defeat,
By so simple a thing as how to eat.

By the books you choose from a well-
filled shelf,
By these ways and more, you tell on your-
self.
So really, there's not one bit of sense
In an effort to keep up false pretense.

There's no sense in trying to fool the world
into believing you're something that you're not.
The only reason you try to fool the world is
because you're not satisfied with yourself. .
because you have not learned the art of living

with yourself. Therefore, you try to be something else to the world. This has to create a great deal of internal conflict and frustration within you and your self-image.

Let me ask you a question. How many times in your life have you accepted the position or the role of mediocrity? Probably more times than you want to admit. But even though you have accepted the role of mediocrity, you don't really want others to know that you have accepted that rôle because that would indicate to the rest of the world that you have not learned the art of living realistically with yourself. You have not learned the art of reaching the goals and objectives which are truly part of your personality and your self-image.

I overheard a conversation the other day where a Foreman was talking to one of his employees. The Foreman said, "You know something, Joe. You are about the laziest man I have ever seen in my life. Don't you do anything quickly?" The fellow looked up at him and smiled and said, "Yeah, I get tired fast." That man had given up on himself. He had accepted a role of mediocrity. Rather than developing a philosophy of learning to live in order to reach his goals, he had given up to the path of least resistance.

You and I both know that you have goals and objectives which you would like to have reached in life but instead, you have settled for mediocrity. Isn't it amazing that the burning desire to succeed is still present in the inner parts of your mind even though you have ignored it for so long? And doesn't that awakened burning desire continue to cause a conflict within you because you know you're not living up to your fullest potential? And doesn't that, in effect, cause you to become defensive with other people, simply because you are not satisfied with yourself?

I have related several times that it is necessary for you to develop a road map to follow a system. Following are ten steps which will help you believe in yourself. . which will help you learn to live with yourself. . and get more living out of life and more life out of living. Let me again caution you!. . . don't try to accomplish all these steps in one day. Take each step and work on it for one week at a time. In ten weeks you will have developed a philosophy that will permit you to really live with yourself because you will have learned to like yourself. It is a foundation from which to spring forth to achieve higher goals and objectives.

Step 1.

Formulate and stamp indelibly on your mind a mental picture of yourself succeeding. Hold this picture tenaciously. Never permit it to fade. Your mind will seek to develop this picture. Never think of yourself as failing. Never think of yourself as part of mediocrity. Never doubt the reality of the mental image. Doubt is your most dangerous enemy. The mind always tries to complete what it pictures, so always picture success no matter how badly things seem to be going to the time. Always realize that the responsibility lies within YOU. not someone else!

Step 2.

Whenever a negative thought, idea or suggestion concerning your personal powers come to mind, deliberately voice a positive thought to cancel out and replace the negative thought. The mind will accomplish what you concentrate on. So when you have a · negative feeling about your job, another individual, yourself. . . get rid of it! Get rid of it right now and replace it with a positive thought.

Step 3.

Do not build obstacles up in your imagination. Depreciate every so-called obstacle. Minimize them. Difficulties must be studied and efficiently dealt with in order to be eliminated. But they must be seen for what they are! They must not be inflated by thoughts of fear. Let me share with you a secret about yourself that you may not know. Your fears, anxieties, and frustrations, **whether real or imagined,** will produce the same physiological responses. If you were walking down a dark alley and you thought someone was going to jump out and get you, there would be certain physiological responses. Your blood pressure would go up, your heart would beat faster, your mouth would get dry, the palms of your hands would become moist. All of those symptoms will occur the same as if someone really did jump out and scare you. So always bear in mind the fact that **imagined** fear is just as deteriorating as **real** fear. Your nervous system can only respond to your thoughts, be they real or be they imagined. Your thoughts, therefore, must be positive!

Step 4.

Do not be awe-struck by other people and try to copy them. Nobody can be **you** as effectively as **you** can be **you**. I said to you earlier that you are not superior, you are not inferior, you are YOU. Most people, despite their confident appearance and demeanor are often as scared as you are and as doubtful of themselves as you may think you are. Don't try to be someone else. Be yourself with all your strength, all your stamina, all your desires, all your goals, and all your successes. You will succeed because you are **you**, not because you appear to be like someone else.

Step 5.

Ten times a day repeat these dynamic words:
"If God be for us, who can be against us?" The Bible tells us very clearly that God wants us to prosper and be successful. Let's not fail Him.

Step 6.

Get a competent counselor to help you understand why you do what you do. Learn the origin of your inferiority and your feelings of self-doubt. They may have started in your childhood, or they may have developed later in life, but in any case, you must deal with them. Self-knowledge leads to understanding and understanding leads to cure. It's also important that you not only understand, but through the counseling sessions you will develop a plan of action, a road map to follow, to lead you to new successes. What you have been up to now is not nearly as important as what you're going to be from this moment on.

Step 7.

Ten times each day practice the following affirmation, repeating it out loud if possible: "I can do all things through Christ which strengtheneth me." Those magic words from St. Paul are the most powerful antidote on earth to inferiority feelings and will assist you in learning the art of how to live with yourself.

Step 8.

Make a true estimate of your own abilities and then raise it ten per cent. Do not become egotistical, but develop a wholesome self-respect. Believe in your own God-blessed powers and then produce them through a plan of action.

Step 9.

Put yourself in God's hands. To do that, simply state, "I am in God's hands." Then believe you are now receiving all the power you need. Feel it flowing into you. Affirm that: "The kingdom of God is within you."

Step 10.

Remind yourself that God is with you and nothing can defeat you. Believe that you now have received power from Him. You know he told us in the Holy Bible that we should love our neighbors as ourself. And if we have not learned the art of living with ourselves, if we have not learned the art of self-love, it is impossible for us to love others.

If you will take these ten steps and apply them to your daily life, make them part of your goals, list the actions necessary to accomplish them, list the attitudes required to make them become a reality, you will discover that you will not only be able to live with yourself, but you will love yourself. And once you are able to live with yourself, and love yourself, you will be able to live with all mankind peacefully.

There is another tremendous secret to becoming a Mental Millionaire which also has to do with learning to live with yourself. Many people have not learned to live with themselves because they do not **want what they have.** It's far more important for you to **want** what you have than to **have** what you want! There's nothing wrong with the couch in the living room. . it's not worn out. . the springs are not coming through the cushions. . but all of a sudden, we 'want a new couch. Ours is out of style and we want to brighten up the room. We have something we don't want, and we want something we don't need. There is nothing wrong with our automobile. It still runs fine. But all of a sudden we want a new automobile. And we rationalize the fact that ours is three years old. . it has 50,000 miles and may cause us trouble. But the truth of the matter is we just don't want it anymore. . we want a new one. We have become a society that basically doesn't want what we have. And that's sad.

Because for many people, if they don't want what they have, then they're not happy with what they are, because in their perceptual world they ARE what they possess. Therefore, if they don't like what they possess, then they don't like what they are!

This does not mean you shouldn't want new things. You SHOULD want new things. But the individual that has learned to become a Mental Millionaire has learned to want what he has. And by wanting what he has, he develops the ability to get what he wants. He knows how to make the most out of what he has. I know a guy that speaks twelve different languages. There's only one problem. . he lies in all of them. He's not utilizing his talents and making the most out of what he has. He hasn't learned to live with himself and, therefore, he spends his lifetime trying to con other people.

Your greatest failure is your failure to try. The failure to make the most out of what you have. It's not how many times you get knocked down. . . it's how many times you get up that really counts. As Albert Einstein once said, "Imagination is more important than what you possess." You are not what you possess. . . you are what you think!"

Many times it will appear to you that there is no way you can possibly be successful in a given situation. And yet, if you make the most out of what you have, you'll discover time and time again that you do come out on top.

Jesus gave various examples of the people who had talents and what they were able to do with those talents. The important thing is not whether you have five talents or two talents or one talent, but are you using the talents which you have? If you've learned the art of using the talents which you have, then you have learned the art of living with yourself. Making the most out of what you have is far more important than having a lot but not making the most of it.

Maybe a little humor will help illustrate this point. I'm reminded of the story of the farmer and the professor who were traveling on the train from Kansas City to St. Louis. As they were riding along, the professor said to the farmer, "Look, we've got a long ride ahead of us so let's do something to help spend the time." The farmer said, "Fine, what would you like to do?" The professor said, "I'll tell you what. I'll ask you a question and if you can't answer it, you give me a dollar, and then you ask me a question and if I can't answer it I'll give you a dollar." Well, the farmer thought about that for awhile and then he turned to the professor and said, "Sir, that doesn't hardly seem parity to me because, after all, you are a college professor and I'm just a farmer, and you're much more intelligent than I. But I'll tell you what I will do. I'll ask you a question and if you can't answer it you give me a dollar. Then you ask me a question and if I can't answer it, I'll give you fifty cents. The professor said that seemed reasonable so he agreed to it. So the farmer looked at him and said, "Tell me, sir, what has four legs, horns and purple fur?" The professor thought and thought, but since he couldn't come up with an answer, he laid the dollar bill down. The farmer quickly picked it up. The professor said, "Wait a minute. What has four legs, horns and purple fur?" The old farmer reached in his pocket and laid down fifty cents, looked at the professor and said, "I'll be durned if I know." That joke may be an example of how one can make the most out of what they have.

But, seriously, you and I live in a world filled with people. No man is an island. He must live, work and communicate with other human beings. Therefore, to help you get the most out of what you have and to assist you in learning how to live with yourself, I have listed some points for you to ponder and place into your system.

* Do more than exist . . . . .Live

* Do more than smile . . . . : .Laugh

* Do more than receive . . . . .Give

* Do more than touch . . . . .Feel

* Do more than look . . . . .Observe

* Do more than read . . . . .Absorb

* Do more than hear . . . . .Listen

* Do more than think . . . . .Ponder

* Do more than talk . . . . .Say
                                      Something

* Do more than petition . . . . .Pray

The more you learn to live with yourself, the better you can live with others. Here are some Do's and Don'ts of communication that will assist you in making the most out of what you have. They will also aid you in learning how to live with yourself.

DON'Ts

1. Don't argue, interrupt or contradict another person while they are talking. Develop the skill of listening until they have finished expressing their ideas.

Interrupting another person while they are communicating always damages their ego. It makes them feel that what they have to say is not important.

2. Don't give advice unless someone asks for it, and then give it sparingly. Persons seeking advice usually only want you to agree with them. But if you do give advice and give it sparingly, you must be willing to accept the responsibility for the advice you have given.

3. Don't take sides in a dispute until you have heard both parties. We all live in perceptual worlds and we perceive situations differently. Make certain that you gather all the facts before you comment.

4. Don't gossip. It's easy to gain attention this way but your listeners will always wonder what you're saying about them when they're not around to hear it.

5. Don't discuss your children's funny sayings unless you're talking to their grandparents. Your children are extremely important and valuable to you, but their experiences may not be nearly as motivating to others.

DO's

1. Do ask for someone's opinion. The

greatest flattery in the world is to ask someone for their opinion. This shows them and tells them that you have confidence in them as an individual.

2. Do be cheerful and optimistic. Another person may want to tell you his troubles, but he doesn't want to hear yours. Someone once said that when we start telling other people our problems, 80% of the people are probably glad we got them and the other 20% don't care. So, as the Holy Bible says . . . "Work out your own salvation."

3. Do poke a little fun at yourself. This keeps us from being stuffy. Let the other person have the last laugh. It's amazing when you're willing to laugh at yourself and strip away some of your veneer, how quickly others will strip away their veneer and let you see themselves more clearly.

4. Do show an occasional imperfection. People really don't like perfection in others. It makes them feel inferior. Don't be ashamed to show a few flaws for then you'll win empathy with people.

5. Do make the other person feel important. This is done by practicing all the things mentioned above.

Learn How To Live With Yourself

There! You have some Do's and Don'ts that will help you get along better with other people, and if we get along better with other people, that is an indication we get along well with ourselves. Let me close this chapter by reiterating something I shared with you earlier. Your biggest problems in the world are not with your husband, or your wife, or your boss, or with other people. Your biggest problems are with yourself! If you will take the time to learn to live with yourself and to make the most out of what you have, you will be amazed at how much eaiser it is to live with other people. "Peace I leave with you, My peace I give unto you . . ." Take it--it's free! Learn to live with yourself.

CHAPTER 5

THE DAY YOU DO NOT LIVE TODAY
YOU'RE NEVER GOING TO LIVE AGAIN

*"Boast not thyself of tomorrow;
for thou knowest not what a
day may bring forth."*
Proverbs 27:1

The Psalmist said, "This is the day the Lord hath made, I will rejoice and be glad in it." One of the fundamental principles the Mental Millionaire understands is this . . . Whatever you're doing today, make it worthwhile for you are giving up one day of your life for that activity. Our yesterdays are gone and, hopefully, we have learned from them. Our tomorrows shall reap the harvests of today's sowing. Yesterday is gone and tomorrow may never come. We have only today to live!

Jesus gave us one of the laws of success when he said, "As ye sow, so shall ye reap." As a Mental Millionaire you should strive to start each day with possibility thinking . . . anticipating only good things.

Remember as a child you learned a little prayer that started out, "Now I lay me down to sleep, I pray the Lord my soul to keep?" Here is this little poem paraphrased as a way to start your day. It comes through practice and patience, but say it every morning.

Now I wake me up to work,
I pray the Lord I will not shirk.
If I should die before tonight,
Then I pray the Lord my work's alright.

The Day You Do Not Live Today . . .

It's amazing how this little poem can start each day off with possibility thinking . . . The thinking that will create for you the attitude and philosophy of becoming a Mental Millionaire. Rest assured that every day is not going to be exactly as you desire it to be. Every day is not going to be a perfect day. But temporary defeat will be a stepping stone or a stumbling block, depending upon the way you react to it. As someone said, "It takes a rough sea to make a good sailor." But far more important than what happens to you in life is your attitude about what happens to you.

I read a sign in a department store the other day that said, "Today is the first day of the rest of your life." How true that is! What you have been up to this point may not matter nearly as much as what you are going to become from this day forward. There are two days in every week about which you should not worry . . . two days which should be kept free from fear and apprehension. One of those days is yesterday with its mistakes and its cares, its faults and its blunders, its aches and its pains. Yesterday is forever beyond your control. You should simply learn from the experiences of yesterday. All the money in the world cannot bring back yesterday. You cannot undue a single act which you performed. You cannot erase a single word you said. Yesterday is gone! Therefore, learn from its experiences and remember those things which were good. Forget those things which were unpleasant.

The other day you should not worry about

is tomorrow, with its possible adversities, its burdens, its large promise and possible poor performance. Tomorrow is also beyond your immediate control. Tomorrow's sun will rise either in splendor or behind a mass of clouds. But it will rise! Until it does, you have no stake in tomorrow for it is yet unborn. This is not to say, however, that you should not plan. The seeds you sow today will be the harvest you reap tomorrow, should the good Lord permit you to see that tomorrow.

This leaves only one day . . . Today! Jesus said, "Today is the day of Salvation." You can fight the battles of life for just one day. Just twenty-four small hours. It is only when you add the burdens of those two awful eternities, yesterday and tomorrow, that you break down. It is not the experiences of today that drive you mad. It is remorse or bitterness for something that happened yesterday and the dread of what tomorrow might bring that causes you to falter and give way to the pressures of life.

If you try and live your life with one eye on yesterday and one eye on tomorrow, that's going to give you a pretty cock-eyed view of today.

You must always learn to be extremely cautious not to build on all tomorrows. If you do, you'll end up with a lot of empty yesterdays that had no production and no seed-sowing. The day to live is today! Come what may, you must get the most out of every day that you live. You must get the most living out of life and the most life out of living.

You must develop the "Do It Now" phil-

osophy! You must become a TNT person . . .
that is, Today Not Tomorrow. The future is
but the today of tomorrow. Live today to its
fullest extent because today is the future of
yesterday. You must live positively in order
to make every moment of this day count.

My wife and I just finished a cruise in the
Caribbean. Each day of that cruise was a glorious, relaxing event. But you know something?
. . . I was ready to come back to work. That's
one of the wonderful things about a vacation.
That on each end of that vacation is work. We
may have a tendency from time to time to
grumble about the performance we must do to
earn our living, but what would we do if we
weren't able to work? This poem will help
illustrate how we can get the most out of each
day that we live.

> How true it is when I'm sad
> A little work can make me glad.
>
> When frowning care comes to my door
> I work awhile and fret no more.
>
> I leave my couch harassed with pain,
> I work, and soon I'm well again.
>
> When sorrow comes in vain regret
> I go to work and soon forget.
>
> Work soothes the soul when joy departs
> And after, mends a broken heart.

The Day You Do Not Live Today . . .

The idle mind soon fills with mirk
So that's why God invented work.

Are you like a lot of people today who get involved in what I call the "Activity Trap"? Do you spend a lot of time doing nothing? Do you aim at nothing and hit it with amazing accuracy? Your success depends, in essence, upon the results which you are able to obtain through your daily activities. If you don't sow seeds, you can't possibly expect to cultivate a harvest.

As discussed earlier, you must develop a system with a plan of action. I'd like to develop another system with you right now because again I feel that the thought process is of no value until it is put into action. Let's look at the following system with ten steps which is a plan of action enabling you to get the most out of every day that you live.

Step 1. JUST FOR TODAY I'll try to live through this day only and not tackle my while life's problems at once. I can do something for twelve hours that would appall me if I felt I had to keep it up for a lifetime. But for twelve hours, I can withstand almost anything.

Step 2. JUST FOR TODAY I will be happy. This assumes to be true what Abraham Lincoln said, "Most folks are as happy as they make up their minds to be."

Step 3. JUST FOR TODAY, I will adjust myself to the reality of what is and not try to adjust everything to my own desires. I will take my experences as they come and fit them into my daily system for success.

Step 4. JUST FOR TODAY I will try to strengthen my mind. I will study. I will learn something useful. I will not be a mental loafer. I will read something that will require effort, thought and concentration. One idea a day will give me 365 new ideas in one short year.

Step 5. JUST FOR TODAY I will exercise my soul in three ways.

a) I will do somebody a good turn and not be discovered. (If anybody knows of it, it will not count).

b) I will do at least two things I don't want to do just for the exercise of accomplishing the task.

c) I will not show anyone that my feelings are hurt. (They may be hurt, but today I will not show it). I will not become defensive today.

Step 6. JUST FOR TODAY I will be agreeable. I will look as good as I can. I will dress becomingly. I will talk in a low voice. I will act courteously. I will criticize no one. I will find fault with no one. I will not try to improve or regulate anybody except myself. I will be a coach instead of a critic.

Step 7. JUST FOR TODAY I will have a program--a system--a plan of action. I may not follow it exactly, but I will have it. I will save myself from two pests . . . "hurry" and "indecision".

Step 8. JUST FOR TODAY I'll have a quiet hour all by myself and relax. During this hour I will try to get a better perspective of my life, my attitudes, my actions and my goals.

Step 9. JUST FOR TODAY I will not be afraid. I will especially not be afraid to enjoy what is beautiful and to believe that as I give to the world, so the world will give back to me.

Step 10. JUST FOR TODAY I wil develop a closer relationship with my God. I will endeavor to follow the examples and precepts which He relates in His Holy Word.

All of these things I will do . . . JUST FOR TODAY.

The Greek Philosopher, Plato, said, "The first and best victory is to conquer self. To be conquered by self is of all things most shameful and vile." How do we conquer self? By learning to live life to its fullest extent each day. By learning to get the most living out of every day that we

live. By learning to live peaceably with ourselves and with others.

Procrastination is one of the greatest killers
of all time. Earlier, I challenged you to become
a TNT person . . . Today Not Tomorrow. How
much more you could accomplish in your lifetime
if you would only do what you know needs to
be done. There are many benefits to be gained
by becoming a TNT person . . . by doing something today that you could put off until tomorrow. And when you analyze these benefits listed
below, you will undoubtedly make the decision
to become a TNT person.

1. You'll have a new feeling of self-
   confidence and courage. Nothing moti-
   vates one to succeed like a successful
   experience. The more successful experiences you can encounter, the greater will
   become your self-confidence and courage.

2. You'll gain more confidence as you do
   the duties you have to perform. Do the
   most disagreeable first. By doing the
   hardest and most disagreeable task in the
   beginning, the tasks that lie ahead will
   appear easier.

3. You will naturally get more done. You
   will increase your efficiency and effective-
   ness.

4. You will become a doer and not a "put-er
   off-er". You will be utterly amazed how

quickly people will begin to identify you as an individual who performs.

5.   You will overcome a lot of fear. Emerson once wrote, "Do the thing you fear, and the death of fear is certain." Many of your fears in life come simply because you have not taken the time to experience certain situations. If you fear doing something, go ahead and do it anyway, and the fear will dissipate.

6.   You will learn to control your actions better and more easily. Each experience that you encounter will provide you with a building foundation upon which to accomplish other feats.

7.   You will receive greater satisfaction, experience, job advancement, salary increases, and develop better attitudes. Nothing succeeds like success!

Now . . . there are ten down-to-earth guidelines for applying this success action system to becoming a TNT person in order to live each day to its fullest potential.

1.   Do something today you **could** put off until tomorrow.

2.   Try doing this early in the day, or the last thing in the evening, or both.

3. Attack the task with vigor, vim and vitality.

4. Do the task without expecting any payment or reward except personal satisfaction from knowing the task has been accomplished.

5. Learn something new every day of your life.

6. Make a new friend each day.

7. Go the extra mile every day. Do a little more than is expected of you. Make an extra sales call, wait on an extra customer, service an extra client, prepare a special dinner, etc.

8. Read and study your Bible daily. Remember that prayer is Man talking to God, and the Bible is God talking to Man.

9. Spend a few moments each day renewing your mind. This can be done only through isolation and meditation. Ten minutes a day will make a difference in your life. What's it going to be . . . meditation or medication? The choice is yours.

10. Outline tomorrow's activities tonight. This way you will have a guideline, a road map to follow for the next day's

activities. It will cause you to cease procrastination and increase performance tremendously.

If you will utilize the "do it now" philosophies discussed in this chapter . . . if you will become a TNT person . . . you will get the most living out of every day of your life.

Once again . . . the day you do not live today, you're never going to live again.

> "This is the day the Lord hath
> made . . . rejoice and be glad in it."

> Forget each kindness that you do
>   As soon as you have done it.
> Forget the praise that falls to you
>   The moment you have won it.
> Forget the slander that you hear
>   Before you can repeat it.
> Forget each slight, each spite, each sneer,
>   Wherever you may meet it.
> Remember all the happiness
>   That comes your way in living;
> Forget each worry and distress,
>   Be hopeful and forgiving.
> Remember good, remember truth,
>   Remember heaven's above you
> And you will find through age and youth
>   True joys, and hearts to love you.

> —Author Unknown

CHAPTER 6

ALWAYS SET NEW AND INTERESTING GOALS FOR YOUR LIFE

"I can do all things through Christ which strengtheneth me."
Philippians 4:13

Emerson once wrote, "The world makes way for a man who knows where he's going." The tragedy of that statement is that so few people really do know where they are going. Few people have developed a system, laid out a plan of action, and designed a road map to follow. We must set goals if we plan to become successful. We must have a specific destination, accomplishment or possession, tangible or intangible. Many times we create goals in our minds as thoughts or ideas but we never do any more about it.

Goals must be put into writing. Goals can be long range, intermediate or short range. But regardless of the length of time involved, they must be specific.

Unfortunately, a lot of people confuse general goal-setting with specific goal-setting. For example, a person may say, "I want to become a better Christian." That really isn't a goal at all. At least it's not a goal that will be accomplished because it lacks definite guidelines. A specific goal is, "I'm going to spend fifteen minutes a day reading the Bible and in one year I will have read it completely through. As I read the Bible, I'm going to put into practice those examples and philosophies I have studied." In these two examples, you see the difference between the specific, or definite, goal and a general goal, or a vague wish or desire.

When you start talking about goals, there are several decisions which you must make concerning goals. You must decide in what you believe. You must decide what you want out of life. You must decide what you're willing to contribute to life in order to attain your goals. This is your beginning . . . your foundation. Every successful person becomes successful by setting definite goals and working hard to attain them. There is no easy way to be successful. Being successful requires hard work. There is no magic formula, no pill you can swallow to make you successful. You must plan your work and then work your plan. One of the outstanding rewards of setting definite goals is the personal happiness you will attain when you achieve those goals and, thus the success that you are so diligently seeking.

You will discover that some of the greatest satisfactions and rewards are in becoming what you want to become . . . in achieving what you desire . . . in accumulating what you want to have while appreciating what you already possess. Are you asking enough of life? People tend to rise to meet demands that are placed upon them. Therefore, it's important that you set your goals high. Be realistic, but reach high!

> I bargained with life for a penny
> And life would pay no more.
> However, I begged at evening
> When I counted my scanty store.

For life is just an employer
He'll give you what you ask.
But once you set the wages
Then you must bear the task.

I worked for a menial hire
Only to learn dismayed
That any wage I would have
asked of life,
Life would have willingly paid.

You must make a decision. What do you want out of life? Jesus said, "Ye have not because ye ask not." That's what a goal is all about. A goal is, first of all, deciding what you want to become or what you want to achieve. You must make a commitment to your goals, work out your plan to achieve those goals, and then stick to it.

Unfortunately, 98% of the people in the world will not take a stand, will not make a commitment, will not set definite goals and then strive to achieve them. Instead, they want to straddle the fence, being able to go one way or the other, depending upon which way they feel would be most advantageous to them. That 98% of the population that takes the fence approach have developed attitudes much like the Southern politician, illustrated in the following story.

The newspaper man approached the politician and asked him this question. He said, "Sir, how do you stand on the whiskey question?" Well, the politician realized he was in trouble because if he said he was FOR whiskey he'd probably get half the votes and lose half of them, and if he said he was AGAINST whiskey, he'd probably lose half the votes and get half of them. Since there were only two in the race, the politician realized he was in trouble. So he thought for a moment, and this is the answer he gave the newsman:

"Sir, I had not planned to discuss that controversial issue at this time. However, I do not plan to sidestep any issue regardless of the nature of the result. But I want to be sure, sir, that I understand exactly what you said. If, sir, when you say 'whiskey', you mean that devil's brew, that poisonous scourage, that bloody monster that defies innocence, dethrones reason, creates misery and poverty, yea takes the food out of the mouths of babes. If you mean that vile drink, sir, that topples the Christian men and women from the pinnacles of righteous and gracious living, puts them in the bottomless pit of despair, hopelessness and helplessness, breaks up homes, creates orphans and deprives the community in general. Now, sir, if that's what you mean by whiskey, I want you to tell my constituents that I will fight to destroy the demon with all the power that I possess.

"But if, sir, on the other hand, by 'whiskey' you mean that oil of conversation, that philosophical wine and ale which when good fellows get together puts a song in their hearts, laughter on their lips and a warm contentment in their eyes . . . Sir, if you mean that drink that puts the spring in an old man's step on a frosty morning, if you mean that nectar of the gods, the sale of which puts untold millions in our treasury, provides money for the orphans, the aged, the maim, the halt and the blind; helps build better schools, hospitals, highways and things which make this a better place in which to live . . . Now, sir, if that's what you mean by 'whiskey', I want you to put in your paper that I promise my constituents that I will fight this right to divinity with all the power that I possess.

"And now, sir, that I have answered your question without any equivocation or mental reservation, I want you to put in your paper that I am a man of my convictions. I will not . . . I say I will **not** compromise. This is my stand."

Humorous? Yes . . . to a point. But, unfortunately, that's the way many people look at life if they really don't want to be successful. Why? Because they want to straddle the fence. In essence, they don't want to make a commitment.

Always Set New and Interesting Goals . . .

And making a commitment is what setting goals is all about. You must decide wherein your commitments are going to lie. And you must do it in terms of setting specific goals. You must make decisions concerning your commitments to life.

> I saw them tearing a building down
> A gang of men in my home town.
> With a heave and a ho and a mighty sound
> They swung a beam and a wall fell down.
>
> And I said to the foreman,
> "Are these men skilled
> As the ones you'd use
> If you had to build?"
>
> He laughed and said, "Oh no indeed,
> Commonest labor is all I need.
> For I can destroy in a day or two
> What has taken a builder two years
> to do."
>
> And I said to myself as I went my way,
> "Now which of these roles am I willing
> to play?
> Am I one who is seemingly tearing down
> As I carelessly make my way around?
>
> Or am I one that's building
> With a great deal of care
> So my community will be better
> Because I am there?"

You must make a commitment. You must decide. Are you going to build up, or are you going to be like the 98% that tear down? In the Dale Carnegie Course they teach you to learn to live by the Three C's.

Never: Criticize, Condemn or Complain.

That sounds difficult. But the longer you work with that system, the easier it becomes. You must establish positive goals for constructive purposes. You cannot develop a philosophy of tearing down if you expect to become a Mental Millionaire. You have to make a commitment . . . a commitment to yourself, to your family, to your community, to your God.

I once saw a sign that I will never forget.

> "At every crossway on the road that leads to the future, each progressive spirit is opposed by a thousand men appointed to guard the past."

There are going to be those who will say to you, "Why establish goals? They won't work. I've tried it. It just doesn't work! Why try to become a Mental Millionaire? Why try to be successful?" WHY? Because you want to be part of the 2% that rises above the mediocrity of society. You want to be an individual who sets specific goals, develops a system to achieve those goals, and then makes a commitment to succeed.

I know many people are content to be average. But I'm certain you're not one of those or you wouldn't be reading this book. You want to climb higher in the successful pattern of living and enjoy each day that you live. You want to learn to live with yourself and be able to set goals and achieve them. The person who's content with being average just doesn't realize that when they are average, they are just as close to the bottom as they are to the top. They are the best of the lousiest and the lousiest of the best. Your goals and desires and dreams are much higher than that.

A definite commitment on your part will be the starting point of your final accomplishments. You're standing on the threshold of achievement when you start with the desire to go forward. Go to the Holy Bible and read the commandment that God gave to Moses. It was simply this . . . "Go forward!"

If you're worrying about failure, remember if you never fail you'll probably never learn. To never fail oftentimes indicates that you are operating within your capabilities, or below them. The challenge is to see if you can go beyond your capabilities. Stretch you abilities as much as you can. Take a giant step forward.

A budding desire is the beginning of everything great. Its absence is the root of decay. Every goal and every achievement, no matter what its purpose, must spring from an intense desire and commitment for something specific. You are created with a nature that when wrapped in strong desire and commitment ignores the word "impossible" and frets not over the prospects of momentary failures. Desire and commitment, when mixed with faith, have inspired many men and women to ignore their circumstances and carry on to greatness and wealth; to really believe what St. Paul meant when he said, "I can do all things through Christ which strengtheneth me."

One of the most interesting things about great men is that in most instances their natural abilities are no greater, or perhaps even subordinate, to the abilities you possess. Your natural abilities and assets, when coupled with an intense desire to achieve and a commitment to follow through, will carry you far beyond the horizons of success experienced by the average man.

Regardless of your intelligence, innate abilities or good intentions, you will not succeed in accumulating wealth or becoming a Mental Millionaire, or anything else worthwhile, unless you are working a practical plan. You will never control your circumstances until you have learned to control yourself. There has never been a great man who blamed his momentary failures on circumstances. Nor has any man become great by allowing circumstances to control him. What do you want from this life? Whatever it may be, you must formulate a practical and sound plan for achieving your goals, and then exercise persistence in working that plan. Napoleon Hill said, "No one is ever whipped until he quits in his own mind."

Henry Ford amassed a fortune because he had a sound plan. He refused to be swayed by temporary defeat. Thomas Edison failed many times before he perfected the electric light bulb. Temporary failure can only mean one thing . . . Your present plan or system is not entirely sound.

There are some inconsistencies which are out of control that you must go back and work on.

When your present plan or system of action fails, it is not a signal for you to give up. It is time to rebuild your plan, re-establish your goals and continue on toward success. In evaluating your plan keep one thing in mind . . . To become a Mental Millionaire, to receive wealth, to achieve your goals . . . you must always render an equivalent service. Our free enterprise system insures that you will have the opportunity to gather riches--those of monitary value, spiritual value and mental value--which will be in direct proportion to the service you render.

Your goals must have a plan of action. The following Three-Step System is a plan of action that will help you move toward success.

First of all, get some paper and a pencil and list three goals you wish to achieve this year . . . just three.

Secondly, now that you have listed the goals, list the actions you feel are necessary to achieve them. What actions, what type of performance, what must you do in order to achieve those goals? Are you going to have to increase sales calls? Are you going to have to start work an hour earlier and stay an hour longer? What actions do you perceive are necessary to achieve those goals?

Thirdly, make a list of the attitudes you feel are necessary to let you take the action to achieve the goals. Let me go over those again.

First, list three goals you want to achieve. Secondly, list the actions that will achieve those goals . . . and thirdly, list the attitudes that will allow you to take the action to reach the goals.

Many individuals spend a lifetime trying to discover their talents. You might hear them make comments like this . . . "If only I could find my niche in life. If only I could really find out what my talents are." Let me make a vital point . . . One doesn't find his talent, nor does one discover his talent. One **decides** on his talent. And then with a plan of action, a system, pursues that talent. Once you have decided on what your talent will be, you must train that potential power within you until it is fully developed. The world today is full of two types of people. Those who are decision makers, and those who are non-decision makers. And God help the non-decision makers . . . because basically they can't help themselves. If you're going to be successful, you must become a decision maker. Don't try and **find** your talent. **Decide** on it. And then go do it. How do I become a decision maker? Very simply. By making decisions!

Let's take a look at a few facts. There are 8,760 hours in a year. Assuming that we have eight hours for work and eight hours for rest, that still leaves us a total 2,920 hours to do what we want. Think of that for a moment . . . 2,920 hours you had last year to do with as you pleased. What did you accomplish with those 2,920 hours? Did you establish goals? Did you set up plans of action? Were you able to achieve those goals? 2,920 hours is a lot of time to do a lot of things. Many of you probably didn't accomplish anything unusual with that extra time. But now, because of your present awareness, by becoming

Mental Millionaires, you're going to put those 2,920 hours to work during the next year. You're going to accomplish your goals and your objectives. You're going to move in the direction of becoming successful. It's not difficult when you take it step by step.

If you spend just one hour a day, seven days a week, you will realize 30.1 hours each month to utilize and develop whatever skills you desire. To reach whatever goals you want, all you have to do is utilize 30.1 hours a month. I'll guarantee you that if you spend those 30.1 hours a month on any given subject, at the end of the year you will be a qualified expert in whatever area you have chosen. Sound easy? It is! It's simply a matter of setting your goals, establishing your plan and your system, and following through to completion. One great idea, properly utilizing one hour a day, can revolutionize your work, your life, your attitude, your future, your success and your monetary achievements. Not only is it possible to become a Mental Millionaire with just one good idea, it's possible to become a monetary millionaire . . . and, after all, money is a by-product of attitude.

The mind of an individual can lift anything. Isn't it worth spending that one hour each day developing your future? Don't be a passenger . . . be the engineer. Don't be the caboose at the end of the train . . . be the individual up front who's calling the shots, making the decisions, setting the goals, determining the destination. Put yourself in the driver's seat. It's YOU who must determine your future . . . not someone else!

James Allen wrote in his book, **As A Man Thinketh,** "He who cherisheth a beautiful vision, a lofty ideal in his heart, will one day realize it." That's how goals begin. The accomplishment of your goals begins with the belief that you can and will one day possess them. But if you are going to establish a goal, you must have a system. You must have a plan of action. These five steps will help you accomplish that goal.

Step 1. Decide what you want. What are those goals you are going to establish? Choose only three. Don't try to conquer the world in one great move. Do it a step at a time. "Inch-by-inch, it's a cinch . . . Yard-by-yard, it's hard."

Step 2. Describe your starting point. Whatever you're going to become tomorrow, you have to begin with what you are today. Wherever you're going tomorrow, you have to start from where you are right now. So once you have established your goals, you must decide on a starting point. Let's assume that during the next twelve months you want to save $1,200. What is your starting point? You say you now have zero dollars. Therefore, in order to achieve your goal of $1,200, you must save at least $100 a month for the next twelve months. It's just that simple. That leads us to the third step.

Step 3. Determine what route you will take. The route you're taking in the above example is saving $100 per month to achieve your goal. So for the third point, you must determine what route you will take. You know the starting point, you know the goal, now you have to determine a step by step plan of how to get there.

Step 4. Place a time limit on it. In the example you said you would save $1,200 in twelve months. If you don't put the "twelve months" on it, two years from now I'll almost guarantee you still won't have the $1,200. Whatever goals you are establishing, put a time frame on yourself so you'll be able to measure your progression toward that worthy ideal you have established.

Step 5. Describe all possible obstacles that you may encounter. Write down the things that might cause your plan of reaching your goal to go astray. Simply list those. Don't think too much about them. Just list them. Once you have listed every obstacle that you can possibly think of, go back and intellectually analyze and say, "All right, if point number one were to happen, what would I do?" Now you see, if point one should happen, you have already given thought and consideration to some source of action to take as an alternate route, thereby assuring yourself that you are going to be able to continue on and achieve your goals, rather than throwing up your hands when you meet an obstacle and saying, "That's it, I'm finished."

Albert Hubbard once wrote, "The line between failure and success is so fine that we scarcely know when we pass it. So fine that we are often on the line and do not know it. How many a man has thrown up his hands at a time when a little more effort, a little more patience would have achieved success? As the tide goes clearly out, so it comes clearly in. Sometimes prospects may seem darkest when really they are on the turn. A little more persistence, a little more effort and that seemingly hopeless failure may turn into glorious success. There is no failure except in no longer trying. There is no defeat except from within. There are no real insurmountable barriers, save our own inherent weakness of purpose."

As you live your life, set new and interesting goals, create a plan, and then achieve it. It produces tremendous results and rewards.

CHAPTER 7

HOW TO TURN PROBLEMS INTO PROJECTS

Since there is no such thing as absolute perfection where human beings are concerned, and realizing that we all make mistakes occasionally, we must then have a clear understanding that each and every one of us at various times in our lives are going to face problems. Unfortunately, many times we concentrate on the problem and thereby end up being completely frustrated, disillusioned and disappointed.

There are times when things will not be going right in our personal lives. There are going to be times when we have marital problems. There are going to be times when we have problems with employees. There are going to be times when tools and machinery are going to break down. There are going to be times when as a businessman you might experience a shortage of materials or a lack of manpower, or a drop in morale. Many different, unforeseeable factors may arise. As a result, we have problems.

As long as we concentrate on the problem, we're never going to achieve a solution. Therefore, realizing that we are going to have problems, it behooves us to develop a philosophy of turning our problems into projects. To stop concentrating on the problem and start working on the various solutions.

Naturally, the best way to handle a problem is

to prevent it, because an ounce of prevention is worth a pound of cure. But since we're not always going to be able to prevent problems in every situation, we must turn the problems into projects to keep our frustrations and conflicts at a minimum.

The problems encountered in life come to us in one of two forms . . . either frustration or conflict. Your ability to identify the problem as a frustration or a conflict will be of tremendous value to you in reaching a solution. Let me describe frustration and conflict to a fuller extent.

What is frustration? We hear the word used a lot. People will say, "Oh, I'm frustrated," or "he frustrates me," or "this is a very frustrating situation." In most cases they are using the term "frustration" simply as a means of expressing any problem they are encountering. Whereas, if they truly understood frustration, they would be in a better position to turn the problem into a project.

As an example of a frustrating situation, let's assume you are on your way to work one morning. Your goal is to go from your home directly to work. In a normal day you are able to leave your home and get to work without any problem. But this morning, while you are driving to your destination (to reach your goal), you suddenly have a flat tire. Now, what do you feel? You say, "I feel frustration." And that's right. But why is it frustration rather than conflict? It is frustration because your goal has been blocked by an external source . . . in the case illustrated here, the flat tire. How do you correct the problem and turn it into a project? Very simply. By removing the external source of frustration, the flat tire, putting on the spare tire, and going on to your point of destination to achieve your goal.

Let's take another example. Let's assume that you have an employee working for you. That employee has a goal of being happy today . . . not having problems with anyone. Yet she comes to you during the day and she says, "Mr. Boss, I have a problem and my problem is Susy Q." You discuss the problem with her and discover that because of Susy Q.'s attitude, the employee is upset. In other words, Susy Q. is frustrating this employee. You may sit and counsel with this employee as long as you like, but you are not going to remove the frustration nor are you going to solve the problem until you bring in the external factor which is blocking the goal . . . in this case, Susy Q. Only when you bring in the external factor will you turn the problem into a project. This is the same as when you put the spare tire on the rim to replace the flat tire.

Any time you are dealing with a frustration, it is caused by an external factor. And in order to solve that problem and turn it into a project, you're going to have to get the external factor involved.

Let's look at one more example. A young man in high school who on Tuesday asked his girlfriend for a date for Friday evening, making an assumption that he could borrow his father's car. Now certainly the young man had a plan, the young man had a goal, and he saw a way of achieving that goal. Then as he approaches his father to ask permission for the car, the father relates that he is very sorry but he has made plans . . . he and his wife will be using the car that evening. Now the young man is frustrated. Why? . . . because he can't have a date? No . . . but because his goal of getting the family car was blocked by an external factor, in this case his father. In order to turn that problem into a project, the young man is going to have to work out a solution of either double-dating with someone. else, walking, using public transportation, or finding some other solution. But the point is that in order to get rid of the frustration, he will have to deal with the external factor that caused the frustration.

If, in your various day-to-day problems, you can identify an external factor and realize it is frustration, you're well on your way to turning the problem into a project.

Let's look now at the second type of problem . . . Conflict. Conflict is when an internal problem has arisen and a solution must come from within us. There are no external forces basically involved. A conflictual situation may appear in one of three ways.

First of all, a conflictual situation may appear as an approach-approach situation. This is sometimes referred to as a plus-plus conflict. In this situation as in other conflictual situations, you must make a decision between two factors. Let's say you have done an excellent job during the past year and your Company has decided to reward you. Now, here comes the conflict. They say to you that you may either have a week's paid vacation in Hawaii or you may have a cash bonus. You then start the mental process of solving the problem and you say to yourself, "Oh my, which reward do I want?" You now have a problem. It's a good problem, because either way, you win. It's a plus-plus. But there's nobody else involved. It's you and you alone. You must make the decision between two pleasant alternatives, plus-plus.

The young man in high school knows that two very attractive young ladies would accept his invitation to go to the dance if he were to ask them. The question is, which one will he ask? Both are attractive. Both are pleasant. In either case, he wins. But again, he must make the decision. But either way, he wins.

Let's take a look at a second type of conflict which might exist. This type of conflict we refer to as avoidance-avoidance or a minus-minus conflict. In a minus-minus conflict, either way you lose. For example, we are in the middle of an austerity program and your boss comes to you and explains the situations. He says, "I'm very sorry, but we must cut back on finances and people. Would you rather take a 10% cut in pay or would you rather be terminated on Friday?" Unlike frustration, nobody else is involved. It's a conflict. It's within you. Which one do I want? Actually, with a minus-minus, either way we go we lose. We either lose 10% of our income or we lose our job. So we try to evaluate which would be the best for us. Should we go ahead and lose our job and try to find another one, or should we take a 10% cut in pay and then try to find another job? What should we do? The decision-making process is up to us. We ourselves must turn the problem into a project as we look for solutions. But either way we go with a minus-minus, we lose.

Let's take a look at the third type of conflict. This is the greatest area of conflict. This conflict is called approach-avoidance or a plus-minus conflict. This is where we have both a positive feeling and a negative feeling about the same object. These are much more difficult to resolve than plus-plus or minus-minus conflicts. Given the plus-plus or the minus-minus, we generally can make those decisions rather quickly. But plus-minus usually creates a great deal more anxiety. For example, you may say you love your dog, which is a plus factor, but he chews on household objects, barks unnecessarily, and digs up the yard, which is a minus factor. You have a plus and a minus toward the same object. You then must reach a decision. Do you love your dog enough to put up with the mischief? You may say you really like the Company you work for, that's a plus factor. But you don't care for your supervisor. That's a minus factor. The plus-minus conflict does create within us our greatest anxieties. Our decision-making process becomes much more difficult in a plus-minus than it does in a plus-plus or minus-minus conflictual situation.

The key to all this is your ability to understand that as you encounter problems, you must turn them into projects. Are you dealing with frustration where another party is involved?

Or is this strictly a conflictual problem where the decision must come from within you? If you have the ability to isolate the problem into a frustrated or conflictual area, you are well on your way to turning that problem into a project.

How do you handle a problem once you have identified it? Actually, whether the problem is small or large, there is a system of four basic steps that will assist you in turning a problem into a project. I'll outline this system for you and then cover it in detail.

Step 1. DEFINE THE PROBLEM
    a. Get the background.
    b. Observe the situation.
    c. Talk with other people if they are involved.
    d. Consider the opinions and feelings as facts to be dealt with.
    e. Try to decide exactly what the problem is, separating the symptoms from the problem.
    f. Be sure and get all the facts.

Step 2. ESTIMATE THE SITUATION
    a. Arrange the situation.
    b. Fit the facts together.
    c. Develop at least three solutions.
    d. Consider the effect of each solution on the individual, the group and anyone else involved.
    e. Select your final solution.

Step 3. TAKE ACTION
   a. Consult with someone if assistance is required.
   b. Determine your time schedule for action.
   c. Work with and through others where necessary.

Step 4. EXAMINE THE RESULTS
   a. Watch for changes in individual attitudes, group reactions and group output.
   b. Compare the situation now with what it was at the beginning.
   c. Make adjustments as necessary.
   d. Ask yourself what you have learned.
   e. Keep a record of your progress.
   f. Be willing to pass your findings and information on to others.

There is a system that will work for you if you work the system. It's used by your doctor, by the military officer, by an engineer, by your boss and, hopefully, by you. You must fix your attention on one problem at a time and turn it into a project as quickly as possible.

Let's examine in detail the four basic steps for turning a problem into a project.

Step 1. **Defining the Problem.** The first step in handling any problem is to decide exactly what the problem is. Is it conflictual or is it frustration? Are there others involved or is it you alone that is involved? If you fail to identify the problem, your results will be a waste of time, thought and effort. Identifying the problem is half of the solution. Often, careful investigation of what is believed to be a major problem turns out to be a minor problem. At other times the problem which appears to be a surface type problem may prove to be deeply rooted. You must get the facts! Preconceived notions, misinformation and half-truths are not keys to a real solution. You must assume at the beginning that you do not know the whole story.

Charles Kettering, the famous automobile research wizard once said, "It ain't the things you don't know that will get you in trouble . . . but the things you know for sure that ain't really so." How can you get the facts? By personal observation. By interviewing other people involved. By checking family rules and regulations or Company rules and regulations . . . or whatever the case may be. When you have completed a thorough investigation of these areas, you will have a good "case history" from which to work.

Step 2. **Estimating the Situation.** Once you have defined the problem and completed the case history, you are ready for this step . . . Estimating the situation. If you have examined, arranged and weighed the facts carefully, you are ready to develop possible answers and solutions to the problem, as you turn it into a project. Draw up at least three solutions incorporating your ideas and those of others, if others are involved. The reason for more than one solution is important, yet often overlooked. The first solution you develop is apt to be the most obvious one. But the obvious solutions is not necessarily the best. Approach the problem from all angles and develop solutions.

We have a tendency to go from a problem directly to a solution. Don't do that. Take the time to analyze the facts and estimate the situation. Don't look for extreme or oversimplified answers only. Many individuals tend to move from one extreme to another or fail to analyze the middle ground approach. A sound solution to a problem should enable you to give reasonable, acceptable answers when you ask yourself these three questions:

1. How will it affect the individual(s) involved?

2. How will it affect production or service?

3. How will it affect the group or the family?

If the solution doesn't satisfy these test questions, chances are it's not the real answer.

Step 3. **Taking Action.** Those individuals who are unsuccessful in solving problems generally fall into two types. There is the "hasty action" individual who makes the mistake of thinking that action alone is the key to turning a problem into a project. He is so anxious to take action that he forgets to analyze and he usually comes up with the wrong answers. The second is the "pipe-smoking philosopher" type of an individual. Even after he has several possible solutions, he continues to drag out the deliberation process. He becomes bogged down trying to decide which solution to choose because of trifling differences between them. The result is that he never reaches the Taking Action phase . . . or else he reaches it so late the decision is now of little or no value.

Problem solving requires deliberation (define the problem and estimate the situation) followed by decisive activity (taking action and examining the results). It can be compared with the behavior of a cat who, after quietly stalking his prey and observing it from all directions, finally pounces with great enthusiasm. Once you have decided to take action, you may want to check it out with other people. If your problem is difficult, big, new, or whatever, you may be wise to seek the advice of someone who has expertise in that given field.

The timing is a vital factor when you take action on a problem. You have figured out how it should be done . . . now you must decide when to do it. Should it be today, tomorrow, next week? Perfectly good decisions fail because they are executed at the wrong time. Everyone knows it's foolish to approach the boss for a raise when he is angry, worried or tied up with other matters. The need may be present and justifiable, but the timing certainly is wrong.

It's important that in taking action you work through other people where necessary. Most problems arise because of some human weakness, failure, blind spot, or oversight. This means that in solving them you may have to work with other people. Again, you see the value of open line communications. Once you put the solution into action, be prepared to stand behind it. Don't pass the buck if it doesn't work out! Just because you have consulted with others does not relieve you of the responsibility of the decision. Basically, the decision is yours.

Step 4. **Examine the Results.** Now that your decision has been made and your plan of action has begun, you must observe it in operation to see if it's actually working. You do this by careful examination. Look for changes in attitudes, relationships, or output of individuals involved. Try to gauge the effect of the results on the people who are involved. Has the solution to this problem created new problems? If your solution isn't working out as well as you planned, think about what changes or adjustments might be needed, then don't be afraid to make them. Very seldom will you reach a conclusion that doesn't have "bugs" to be ironed out. If examining the results indicates that you have hit upon an unusually effective solution, you will want to report it to your superiors and those around you that have a need to know.

The difference between success and failure in every walk of life is the fact that the successful person has trained himself to turn problems into projects. The earmark of a good manager, or executive, or husband, or wife, is that person's ability to achieve sound, acceptable solutions to a good percentage of their problems. . . the ability to turn problems into projects with meaningful solutions.

CHAPTER 8

BE ENTHUSIASTIC -- IT'S CONTAGIOUS

Let me share with you something I once heard called, "The Magic in Man." What would you say is the world most priceless element? Is it gold? Is it silver? Is it diamonds? Is it rubies? Is it Uranium 235? None of these! They are precious, but they are not priceless. This particular element that I'm talking about you can't buy, beg, borrow or steal. But if you will build it into your system of life, you will truly discover it is the Magic in Man. It's very rare, yet very contagious. Anyone can get it, but few people have it. In business it rates ahead of professional skills. It is the heart and soul of all religion. It makes hard work enjoyable. It banishes fear. It wins even when desire, ambition, intelligence and opportunity don't seem to be enough.

What is this most precious, priceless, irreplaceable, magical element? It is enthusiasm! Without enthusiasm we are blind, deaf and only half appreciative of the wonders of the world. Without enthusiasm we are little, plain and bland . . only a shadow of our real potential. Nothing. . I repeat, NOTHING . . in this world is accomplished without true enthusiasm. A salesman without enthusiasm is just a clerk. A mother without enthusiasm is just a housekeeper. A father without enthusiasm is just a financial provider. A teacher without enthusiasm is un-inspiring and a real bore. Ability or talent without enthusiasm is like a rifle without a bullet. It's like a motor without gasoline. It's like a light bulb without electricity. Enthusiasm is that wonderful propellent that lifts us out of mediocrity, elevates us above the commonplace, above ridicule, above prejudice and above our fears. Enthusiasm gives you a magnetism that pulls others along with you. It puts vigor in your voice, confidence in your step and creative optimism in your outlook. Trying to stop a person charged with enthusiasm is like trying to still time, silence the thunder, or cap a volcano. It just cannot be done. Do you have the magic of enthusiasm? You certainly do! Do you utilize it? Therein lies the question!

Enthusiasm is the one common characteristic, the one golden thread that is found built into the system of every successful person. It is the most contagious of all emotions. It is the avenue of all spiritual development. Enthusiasm rings as an air of excitement into everything you do in life. It causes you to glow with a radiant feeling of expectancy. Enthusiasm has the same relationship to man that fire brings to a steam boiler. It heats up the powers of the mind and gives you the force of action necessary to accomplish your plan . . to achieve your goals.

This example will help illustrate why I believe so whole-heartedly in the importance of enthusiasm, of conviction, of personal sincerity, of using your full potential. At 211 degrees, water is just water. . . inert, powerless. But at 212 degrees, water becomes live steam with more power inherent than man ever believed possible when he first started experimenting with steam as a source of power. At 211 degrees the water in a locomotive boiler exerts not one ounce of pressure. But at 212 degrees the water in that locomotive exerts enough power to haul a mile-long train of cars across a mountain pass. At 211 degrees, a locomotive is as powerless as if the firebox were empty and cold. But at 212 degrees it has the power to pull a mile-long train of cars rattling along the right-of-way at 90 miles an hour.

Many people are walking around at 211 degrees who, for want of one more degree of temperature, are relatively powerless and far less effective than they should be. There are people walking around at 211 degrees who, if they would but throw one more log on the fire, another lump of coal, could raise their temperature to 212 degrees and increase their power by infinity. That one last degree out of 212 degrees seems insignificant by itself, yet it is of incomparable and everlasting importance. The person who will never lift their temperature to the boiling point may never achieve anything worthwhile in this world. Those who can and will keep their temperature above 212 degrees, who can and will keep their boiler at full steam by using the fire of enthusiasm, can achieve anything in this world to which they may reasonably aspire. Emerson once wrote, "Nothing great has ever been achiev-ed without enthusiasm." This is more than a well-stated literary phrase. It is a road map to achievement . . . a road map to happiness . . . and a road map to success.

How do you get enthusiasm? The answer is very simple. You get enthusiasm by practicing being enthusiastic. What makes an individual a good golfer? Practice! What makes an individual a good artist? Practice! What makes an individual a good linguist? Practice! What makes an individual a good individual? Practice! . . . nothing else! So what makes an individual enthusiastic? Practice, practice, practice!

Enthusiasm is also built by action. For example, our physical actions regulate and change our mental attitudes. Let's say you want to paint a room but you keep procrastinating. Once you finally do start painting and begin to see the results, your attitude changes . . . you develop a great deal of enthusiasm to finish that room and become excited about the final results.

Enthusiasm begins to develop that TNT philosophy we talked about earlier . . . Today Not Tomorrow. Right now is the time!

Here are Ten Personal Benefits you will receive when you practice enthusiasm. They follow enthusiasm just as surely as night follows day.

BENEFITS GAINED BY BEING ENTHUSIASTIC

1. You'll improve your personality.
2. You'll be more comfortable around other people.
3. You'll persuade and influence people with more ease.

4. You'll become more interested in other people and things around you.
5. You'll make friends easier.
6. You'll become a welcome guest in any group.
7. You'll gain more recognition as a leader.
8. You'll learn to express yourself more efficiently, and effectively.
9. You'll feel younger and more alive regardless of your present age.
10. You'll overcome a lot of fear, worry and tension by gaining courage.

Every successful individual I have met in my lifetime that has become a Mental Millionaire was filled with enthusiasm . . . the necessary source of energy to succeed.

CHAPTER 9

HOW TO INCREASE YOUR
SELF-CONFIDENCE

Have you ever felt that if you had a little more self-confidence you might become successful? You feel you really don't know how to gain self-confidence. You've tried . . but nothing really seems to work. This chapter discusses ways in which you can increase your self-confidence. We will begin by taking a look at two men.

One is so ugly and ungainly, people can only compare him to a gorilla. He has less than one year of schoolroom education. His father is a poor farmer. His mother an alleged illegitimate child. His wife a shrew. He enters business and goes bankrupt. He runs for the United States Senate and is defeated. He applies for an appointment at the United States Land Office and is rejected. If ever a man seemed destined to total failure, this man does. Acutely aware of his shortcomings, tormented by doubt as to his ability and frustrated by his failures, he actually contemplated suicide. Yet, he overcame his doubts, his fears, his frustrations and his failures. And as President of the United States of America, he led a divided nation through a real ordeal of fire. As Commander in Chief of the United States Army, Abraham Lincoln attacked the problems of war with surpassing skills and decisiveness and turned those problems into projects. At his death he was even mourned by men who opposed him in life.

Now let's look at the second man . . . a young man from Budapest and almost as tall as Lincoln. He arrived in America at the age of seventeen. . . excessively thin with a rather large head, a pointed chin, a big nose and a marked foreign accent. Although he studied law and passed the bar exam, the twin handicaps of appearance and speech stood in the way of a successful practice. Haunted by the fear of being unable to support himself, half sorry that he left his homeland and, in desperation, he took a job as a Reporter for a German paper in St. Louis, Missouri. Reporters on other papers taunted him about his looks and his speech. A stranger in an alien land, he toyed with the idea of returning to Europe. Yet at 31 years of age, he was Owner and Publisher of the St. Louis Post Dispatch. In the years that followed, Joseph Pullitzer bought the New York World and became one of the greatest and most influential Publishers of all times.

By all rules we should never have heard of this man. We should never have heard of Abraham Lincoln. They apparently had no qualifications to succeed . . but they did! Why?

The answer, of course, includes such factors as hard work, self-discipline, a burning desire to make a wish come true, and a conscious development of the skills they needed to succeed. They both realized that there are few secrets to success. They were able to put together a system that was consistent and well-controlled. They understood that success is doing the things you know you should be doing. Success is focusing the full power of all you have on what you want to achieve. These men realized that success is not arriving at the summit of a mountain, but rather, that success is a perpetual growth. They understood these things. And somewhere along the line, these two men, and thousands like them, picked up the propelling energy and determination that comes from being sure of oneself . . of having self-confidence. They developed the philosophy of becoming Mental Millionaires.

These men -- a President and a Publisher -- belong to an elite segment of our population. . . that fairly small group that makes things happen. It has been said that we have three groups of people in America today -- those who don't know what's happening . . those who watch things happen . . and those who make things happen. It's that small 2% that make things happen. Unfortunately, most people are unsure of themselves, insecure, scared of making up their minds, controlled from without and not from within. For every Lincoln or Pullitzer, there are dozens of others resigned to mediocrity or failure. And the sad fact is that they themselves have chosen that road to mediocrity or failure. Someone else did not choose it for them. Someone else did not force them to walk down that path. Self-confidence, like your vocabulary, is something you can build into yourself. If you're tired of being half-sure . . if you're tired of indecisiveness . . if you're tired of self-doubt . . if you truly want to think, act, feel and look self-confident . . believe, me, you can! It is entirely up to you. . . no one else.

It has been said that the best way to have a good offense is to understand the defense. Why do some men and women lack self-confidence? Why do so many people fall short in this area? Why will they bet freely on horses or dogs or spinning wheels, but seldom bet on themselves? What makes them think they are inferior to their fellow men? What force shapes that 98% who are unsure of themselves and lack the self-confidence needed to step out and become successful?

Below are eight "Confidence Killers" which are usually the culprits that keep you from developing the self-confidence you need to become a Mental Millionaire. If you see any of these eight confidence killers starting to creep into your life, rid yourself of them immediately.

EIGHT CONFIDENCE KILLERS

1. **An unfortunate experience.**
   At one time or another, every one of us has been exposed to an ego-shattering experience. The boss Chews us out. A promotion passes us by. Someone says they don't love us any more. Our friends are starting to gossip about us, etc. From those experiences we draw the generalization that we are unworthy, unskilled, unloved, unattractive or friendless . . and our self-confidence takes a nosedive.

What's the antidote for the first Confidence

Killer? Be rational. No scientist would draw a conclusion from the flimsy evidence of one, two or three experiences or experiments. Hundreds or perhaps thousands of tests would be run before he would be satisfied that his conclusions were valid. The same applies to you. Has your boss been barking? Recall the compliments he paid you in the past. Did that promotion fall through? Look where you are today compared to where you were two years ago. Is your wife unhappy with your performance? Think of all the good times you had during those years of marriage. Don't dwell exclusively on temporary setbacks. Weigh all the evidence and you'll come to the realization that for every unfortunate experience you have in life, you will have ten fortunate experiences to back it up.

2. False Assumptions.

"Charlie never really like me." "When you're born on the wrong side of the tracks, you stay there." "Nobody is interested in my opinion." "Without pull in this old world, you're dead." "It's not what you know, it's who you know." Such a formula of thinking paralyzes initiative and destroys self-confidence in a most confronting way. It takes matters out of your hands. "They" are against you, and that's all there is to it.

Antidote - Recognize such assumptions for what they really are . . . poor excuses. Get on with the business at hand. Think of all the successful people who have risen above their backgrounds. I could give you a long list, and you could share a long list with me. There are many people who have risen above their seemingly unfortunate "backgrounds." Thoughts harbor eventual success or failure. For what you think about, you are certain to become.

3. Lack of Education.

Because you never finished high school or college you feel you couldn't possibly compete with those who have obtained a formal education. You believe you are hopelessly outdistanced by those scholastic scholars. Why then should you have faith in your own abilities? This kind of self-effacement stems from the belief that a diploma is an all-powerful "open sesame" to success.

Antidote - First of all, realize that education is not a label that's won by attending a university for four years. Rather, it is a state of mind. If you have an open and inquiring mind and want to learn, you possess the most important requisites for an educated person. Earlier in this book we suggested that if you will just spend one hour a day, within a year you will be an expert in almost any field. Formal schooling is not the only way to achieve an education. Socrates said, "Whom then do I call educated?" First, those who control circumstances instead of being mastered by them. Second, those who meet all occasions manfully and act in accordance with intelligent thinking. Third, those who are honorable in all dealings. . who treat good-natured persons and things that are disagreeable equal. Fourth, those who hold their pleasures under control and are not overcome by misfortune. Finally, those who are not spoiled by success. Perhaps the best, most significant result of all education is the ability to **make yourself do the thing you have to do when it must be done, whether you like to or not.** It is the first lesson to be learned, and regardless of when a man's training begins, it is usually the last lesson that he learns thoroughly. Each one of you is working on a degree. It is called "The Master of Arts in Living." Whether you pass or fail depends entirely upon you.

4. Pessimistic Friends.

To a large extent, our personalities are shaped by the people we know and visit and work with. Everyone has, at one time or another, caught himself using an expression or a gesture learned from a friend. The same holds true of attitudes. Talk long enough to a pessimist . . the kind of person who sees a beautiful sunrise as the beginning of another miserable day . . and you will soon end up like the character in Little Abner with the perennial little black cloud over his head. A "friend" who consistently complains about his health, his job, his luck, the way people treat him, and the general negative state of the world, is bound to form a "what's the use" attitude towards everything. His attitude is that people are just no good, and that includes him.

Antidote - Avoid professional crepe hangers like the plague, Cultivate the friendship of optimists. An optimist prays to forget, but a pessimist forgets to pray. An optimist isn't hard to spot. He bounces when he walks, he bubbles when he talks, and he knows how to smile. It's a tonic just being around him. He has learned how to count his blessings. We need to be like the little old lady who said, "I only have two teeth, but Thank, God . . they hit."

Too many people in the world are pessimistic. I had the advantage this past week of visiting Jamaica and Haiti. I came away from there with one feeling . . We in America should be extremely thankful for what we have . . thankful that we are not succumbed by the poverty that exists in other places of the world. You and I have a responsibility to help alleviate that poverty. All too often do we criticize, condemn and complain when we have so much for which to be thankful. This poem illustrates my point very clearly.

Today upon a bus I saw
A pretty girl with golden hair.
I envied her, she seemed so gay,
I wished that I could be so fair.

And when she rose to leave
I saw her hobble down the aisle.
She had one leg and used a crutch
And yet she passed me with a smile.

How To Increase Your Self-Confidence

Oh God, forgive me when I whine.
I have two legs and the world is mine.

And then I stopped to buy some sweets.
The lad who sold them had such charm.
I talked with him. He seemed so gay.
If I were late, 'twould do no harm.

And as I left, he said to me,
"Please come again. You've been so kind.
It's nice to talk with folks like you,
For as you see, "he smiled, "I'm blind."

Oh God, forgive me when I whine.
I have two eyes and the world is mine.

Then walking down the street I saw
A pretty child with eyes of blue.
He stood and watched the others play.
It seemed he knew not what to do.

I stopped a moment, then I asked,
"Why don't you join the others, dear?"
He looked ahead without a word
And then I knew he could not hear.

Oh God, forgive me when I whine.
I have two ears and the world is mine.

With legs to take me where I go,
With eyes to see the sunset glow,
With ears to hear what I should know,
Oh God, forgive me when I whine.
I'm blessed indeed, and the world is mine.

Avoid the pessimists like they have the plague.

5. Laziness.

It's easier to sit still than to move. It's easier to keep quiet than to talk. It's easier to dream than to act. It's easier to wish than to perform. But confidence is largely based upon action. If you don't do anything, you will never know what you are capable of doing. And how can you be confident about an unknown quality? People who are lazy, seldom admit it. Instead they, "haven't the time" or they "don't feel up to it right now" or they "can't be bothered with such trifles." Do you recognize yourself in there somewhere? If so, you better apply the antidote right now.

Antidote - Analyze your reasons for inaction. Are they valid or are they false? If false, face up to it. Delay no longer. Take the first step toward your goal today, even if it's only a memorandum or a phone call. Become a TNT person! The important thing is DO IT NOW . . . Today Not Tomorrow. Develop the "do it now" habit and you'll be surprised how much it will develop your self-confidence.

6. Poor Health.

It's extremely difficult to do your best when you're not feeling well. Parts of your body's resources are either out of commission or attending to the business of combating illness. Since self-confidence depends to an extent on the knowledge that you are working at peak performance, sickness is bound to undermine it.

Antidote - See a doctor if that below par feeling persists. A physical and dental check-up should be a semi-annual affair. Get adequate rest, exercise, watch your weight and eat sensibly. Whatever you look like is the result of what has gone through your mouth.

7. Lack of Job Knowledge.
There are few confidence killers as deadly as lack of job knowledge. The man who knows, and knows that he knows, has no hesitations or fears when he's confronted by a situation he is equipped to meet, for familiarity breeds **content**. The man faced by a task beyond his knowledge, however, is foredoomed to failure and hence, shattered self-confidence. How much is there that you do not know about your present job?

Antidote - If possible, take refresher courses in your area of expertise. Acquire the habit of holding informal sessions with your peer group in order to gain additional tips for success. Don't be afraid to ask questions of your supervisor. Most people are willing to share with you their knowledge if you're willing to ask for it. Don't hesitate to learn from your subordinates as well as your superiors. We live in a rapidly advancing technological society. We simply can't stand still. You are either going to proceed ahead or fall behind. In the area of knowledge, there's no such thing as status quo.

8. **Excessive Humility.**
   This frequently stems from the belief that the only alternative is overwhelming pride. Not so! There is a middle ground--self-confidence. The proper appreciation of your worth as a human being. Pride is an over-estimated opinion of yourself with little or no basis in fact. An outstanding example of a supremely confident but by no means proud individual would be Bishop Fulton Sheen. By constantly throwing your short-comings into high relief, excessive humility gives you a distorted picture of your overall ability. Check this out very carefully . . . Do you frequently belittle yourself in front of other individuals?

Antidote - Accept the fact that all people have limitations, including yourself. Don't dwell on your shortcomings. Instead, take a look at your plus side. You'll be refreshingly surprised at your talents and abilities.

You have now learned the Eight Confidence Killers. Now you must learn to avoid them. Remember, you have within you all the abilities, all the powers, all the potentials of becoming an individual **extremely** self-confident. The Gospel of Matthew says, "Lay not up for yourselves trea- sures which moth and rust can corrupt, but lay up for yourselves treasures which are in heaven."

How do we lay up those treasures? By the performances we give, day in and day out. Make your performance filled with self-confidence. Like enthusiasm . . . it's contagious!

CHAPTER 10

LOVE AND MARRIAC

"Therefore shall a man ic...
father and his mother and shau
cleave unto his wife, and they
shall be one flesh."

Genesis 2:24

One cannot possibly talk about the secrets of becoming a Mental Millionaire without talking about our ability to understand the psychological, physiological, sociological and spirtual inner actions which take place during the periods of courtship and marriage.

The song . . . "Love and marriage, love and marriage, they go together like a horse and carriage . . . "certainly illustrates the cooperation which must exist if a marriage is to be a fruitful and meaningful relationship. Unfortunately, many people in America have not applied the technologies nor worked at the task of becoming Mental Millionaires in their love and marriage relationships. Psychologists and sociologists have related to us the fact that today we have may problems within the family . . . that the family as a unit has started to disintegrate.

In order to validate their statements, we need only to look at the statistics. The statistics relate to us that 40% of today's marriages will end in divorce. But in this chapter our attention will be focused on successes, rather than failures . . . on ways we can put together a system that will make our marriage a more meaningful relationship. Our thoughts will be based on understanding, rather than on frustrations and conflicts.

In looking at this rather complex subject matter of love and marriage, we'll divide this chapter into three major categories. The first being those relationships existing during courtship . . . secondly, the steps which are involved in marriage . . . and last of all, what I call "The Ten Commandments of A Good Marriage."

COURTSHIP

Without a doubt some of your greatest experiences and memories have been in the area of courtship . . . that time in your life when you were dating the one you felt you loved so very much. Someone once defined courtship as the period between lipstick and mopstick. But I think there are some very evident behavioral patterns which exist during the period of courtship.

Those of you who are married will be able to identify with the steps involved in courtship. Those of you who have teen-age children will certainly be able to identify the psychological and sociological behavior patterns existing during this period in their lives. Those of you who are in the courtship stage will be able to pinpoint your location.

The first step in the courtship relationship, or what we normally refer to as "love", is called PSYCHIC ELATION. Psychic elation occurs when you have met the "right one" for you. This is a time in your life when everything is simply beautiful. The sun shines a little brighter. The heart beats a little lighter. The world becomes a better place in which to live. It is the beginning of seeing the world through rose-colored glasses. To the student, the professor is suddenly all right. To the teen-ager, his parents are more tolerable. To the adult, while past relationships may not have worked out well, he feels extremely positive that it will work out this time. Your whole world becomes a beautiful "pie-in-the-sky" existence. You never felt better before in your life.

From Psychic Elation, the second basic stage of the courtship period begins. This is OVER-EVALUATION OF THE OBJECT. In this stage the individual sees more in his sweetheart than is really present. A specific example to help illustrate this point would be the young man in college. He comes busting into the dormitory filled with Psychic Elation saying, "I'm in love, I'm in love, I'm in love. The world is great." His fellow students start to question him. "Who's the lucky gal?" As he begins to relate to them the person with whom he has fallen in love, he does so in the vernacular of over-evaluating the object . . . everything about her, to him, seems beautiful. But then the guys begin to question. "Wait a minute . . . she weighs 300 pounds, "or", "She has a big wart on her nose," or, "What's there about her that's so attractive?" His value structures have been distorted by his psychic elation, and he has a natural tendency to over-evalute the object. The things perceived by his classmates are simply not a part of his conceptual world. And at that point in time, they simply do not matter because he is in love.

From there we move to the third stage which is UNDER-EVALUATION OF REALITY. When one is filled with psychic elation and has over-evaluated the object to such an extent that the person's weaknesses simply do not exist, then reality appears to temporarily cease and desist. Logic simply disappears.

A specific example would be two individuals who had fallen in love. During the counseling session I discovered that one of them is of the Roman Catholic faith and the other one is of the Protestant faith. Realizing then the discrepancies which may exist between the two religious beliefs, I began to question them concerning their religious philosophies and under what system they planned to raise their children. I received a rather typical response to that question because of their under-evaluation of reality. Their response was, "Oh, we'll work that out later. We are sure there will be no problems whatsoever."

A second illustration that might help to better clarify this stage of courtship happened when I was counseling two individuals. In the discussion I was trying to discover where they were employed. To make a long story short, it ended up that neither one of the young people were employed and yet they were planning on being married immediately. When I confronted them with the realities of providing a livelihood, paying the rent, buying groceries, etc., their response to me was, "Oh, I'm sure we'll find work in the very near future. It will be all right."

In both situations these individuals completely

under-evaluated the reality of their situation because of this tremendous feeling of love they had for each other. A love that overshadowed logic, reason and reality.

The fourth stage that occurs in the courtship period is FANTASY. To understand the impact of fantasy upon a courtship relationship, you need only to go the attic of your mind and remember your own past experiences. Just think of the fantasies . . . the dreams that you created in your own mind in relationship to that other individual that you loved so dearly. The planning you exercised in your mind to make certain that all the interactions between you and that loved one were a perfect, harmonious relationship.

A good example of how fantasy might work is the example of the young boy in high school. He has spotted the "apple of his eye" and decides to make himself known to her. He goes through a long mental process of fantasies trying to establish the best way to meet her. He lays out a perfect plan whereby he'll get up early the next morning and dress extremely well. He'll be standing next to her locker when she appears. At that point, he goes through his mind's eye and creates the words he will express to her so vividly. Sure enough . . . the next morning he gets up, goes through the routine he's worked out in the fantasy of his mind and he's standing next to the girl's locker. As the young girl appears, she sees him, says, "Hi" and all of a sudden, he's tongue-tied. The reality of the situation has overshadowed the fantasy. But those fantasies do exist and are magnified to a great extent during the courtship. Someone said that anticipation is more rewarding than participation. Maybe that's the part fantasy plays in the relationship of courtship.

We see another stage very prevalent in the courtship period of love, and this stage is SENTIMENTALISM. What a big part sentimentalism plays in the love life of two individuals. Stop and think for a moment . . . I'll bet even today you possibly have a rose pressed in the Bible, or some souvenir from the junior-senior prom which you have placed away neatly because it holds a very special significance. There's a very sentimental attitude about the person you love . . . and a sentimental attitude about the relationships which have existed between the two of you. The experiences you have shared together are experiences the sentimentalistic side of you wants to retain for a lifetime.

The next stage we see during the period of courtship is PSYCHIC DEPENDENCY . . . the need to be in the physical presence of the loved one. This was evident when I taught at the University. A young man would "deliver" the young lady to the classroom door and his conversation might go something like this . . . "Honey, I love you. As soon as this class is over, I'll be waiting right outside the door and we'll go to the Student Union for a coke. Don't worry, I'll be here when class is over." You see the element of psychic dependency? They want to be around that individual with whom they are in love. And that grows and grows and grows. You'll see it manifesting itself in many ways by watching the eye contact as they sit across the table sipping a coke . . . by watching them walk hand-in-hand down the street or across the campus. Psychic dependency is a vital part of that period of courtship.

This leads us to the last point. The stage of SECLUSIVENESS. It's just the two of us . . . nobody else. It's almost like the rest of the world does not exist. We have our own little secrets. We have our X's and our O's at the bottom of our love letters. We have our own terminology that means certain things to just us and nobody else. Nobody else can possibly understand the significant meaning of all those seclusive secret little things you and I have established. They're just for the two of us.

If you analyze very carefully the stages that we have gone through in the courtship of love relationship, you will note that much of what appears so far is somewhat abnormal behavior. I remember giving a speech at the University entitled, "The Neurosis of Love." To a great extent this period of courtship does deal with some neurotic behavior . . . mild neurotic behavior . . . behavior that you and I are permitted to get away with by society only because we are in love. If, in business situations or other social situations, we were to over-evaluate the objects and under-evaluate reality, we would be considered a little off-base. But when it's all applied in the arena of love, society permits us that unique relationship.

It's not whether these are good relationships or bad relationships, but they are universal.

We have discussed them in order that you might better understand the relationships which do exist during the period of courtship. One of the fundamental secrets to becoming a Mental Millionaire is the ability to understand and adjust to each and every given situation.

After one has experienced the various stages of the courtship of love, they may make a decision to get married. This leads us to the various steps which occur in a marital situation. When I think of marriage, I'm reminded of the famous saying of my grandmother. She often said, "Whether a guy ends up with a nest egg or a goose egg depends upon the kind of chick he marries." That may be very true.

Marriage is a good thing. In the Book of Genesis we are told that God saw it was not good for man to be alone so He made him a helpmate. It was a relationship ordained in the beginning of time by Almighty God. He said, "Be fruitful and multiply."

We marry because we are in love, yet there are different kinds of love. If we go back to the Greek language, we have several meanings for the word Love. There is the love of Philia . . . which means the joy of sharing. There is the love of Eros . . . which means physical union. And there is Agape love . . . which means Christ-like love. I like to define love as a "mental and physical attraction in the presence of emotional security."

Now let's look at the various steps in marriage.
MARRIAGE
Now that you have gone through the stages of

of courtship, let's take a look at marriage. Basically there are five steps in a marital situation.

The first step we shall call THE HONEY-MOON. The honeymoon is a continuation of all the stages which we talked about during the courtship. Psychic Elation will be present, the Over-evaluation of the Object will be present, the Under-evaluation of Reality will be present, the Sentimentalism will be present. All of those stages discussed in Courtship will be present during the duration of the honeymoon. The length of the honeymoon will, of course, depend upon the individuals. But, as someone once said, "A good clue to the realization that the honeymoon is over, is when you'd rather see the kitchen in good shape than a good shape in the kitchen."

The second step in the marital process is when **reality** begins to set in. This is when all those little things you have let pass by up to now begin to bug you. Your mate is really not what you thought her to be. You discover she really does have a wart on her nose, as your classmates told you many months ago. This is the time many partners will start having those second thoughts about, "Gee, did I really do the right thing? Maybe this isn't all it's cracked up to be. There are a lot of bills to pay . . . the rent, the heat, the electricity, the groceries. There's more to this marriage thing than first love and physical attraction."

The third step in a marital situation is when we begin to have EGO MAGNIFICATION. This is when we start to pick at little things our mate does that we really don't like. You may remember how you used to hold each other's hand and whisper sweet nothings into each other's ear. Suddenly those things are diminishing. You remember how kind and sweet and understanding your partner used to be . . . you go back and remember how you used to say, "Honey, where do you want to go tonight?" And she'd say, "Oh, I don't care. Wherever you want to go will be fine." And now you're in a situation whereby you both express "true" feelings as to where you really do want to go. So your egos begin to magnify issues.

And all this time you have been eating those eggs which really weren't cooked the way you like them. You put up with them anyway because you were in the honeymoon stage. But finally, during the stage of ego magnification, you say to her one day, "Why don't you learn to cook eggs?" She looks at you and says, "I'll learn to cook eggs just as soon as you learn to hang up your pants and stop putting them on the back of the chair." You come to the realization at that point that the honeymoon is over. Reality has set in and ego magnification has started to take place.

This leads us to the fourth step. Step four is when sexual activity begins to slack off. Much of the physical attraction so prevalent in the beginning of the marriage has started to subside. This is only natural. It occurs in every marital situation. The problem that occurs is, how can you as an individual adjust to that given situation? Your wife may come in and say,

"Honey, it's time to go to bed." You look at her and say, "A little later. Right now I'm watching Monday night football." She looks at you with tears in her eyes and says, "Six months ago you didn't want to watch Monday night football." At this time, you start a process that leads us into the fifth and final step of marriage, which is ADJUSTMENT. This is where you either adjust to each other's idiosyncrasies or your marriage falls by the wayside. This is where you make it or you don't. This is where you either learn the art of adjustment or you begin to criticize and pick apart the mistakes of your mate.

I remember hearing one fellow make a snide remark in a counseling session. He said to his wife, "Your cooking is so bad I have to feed the disposal Alka Seltzer!" Well, that's not the best type of adjustment for any given marital situation.

But many times . . . (here I'm speaking specifically to the gentlemen) . . . we have a tendency to forget the things that helped us win the heart of the fair maiden. Remember how you used to open the car door for her? Now, if you go around to open the car door, she thinks you want her to drive.

Do you realize that the average man shaves 18,000 times in his lifetime? He drinks 22,000 gallons of fluid. He wears out 35 suits, 15 coats, 38 pairs of shoes, uses 500 tubes of toothpaste, has his hair cut 1,500 times, takes 6,000 baths, sleeps 200,000 hours, reads 9,000 books, writes his name 43,000 times, washes his hands 73,000 times, and tells his wife that she's wonderful maybe twice. The period of adjustment is very difficult.

The following poem might describe a way to look at marriage.

> As the covered wagon rolled and pitched
> Along the prairie track,
> One sat looking forward . . .
> While one sat looking back.
>
> One searched the wide horizon
> For a bright and better day.
> And one, the disappointed road
> Till it too slipped away.
>
> As the covered wagon rolled and pitched
> Along the prairie track,
> One sat looking forward . . .
> And one sat looking back.

As you look at marriage and adjustment, are you looking forward? Or are you looking back?

Next, let's talk about the Ten Commandments of Marriage. Each Commandment is like a strand of rope. The more strands you can put together, the stronger the rope will be. The more of these Commandments you can get working for you, the stronger will be your marriage.

1. **Thou shalt realize that marriage is a partnership.** Anyone that says marriage is a 50-50 proposition either doesn't understand their mate or they don't understand frac-

tions. It's a 100-100 proposition! It takes EVERYTHING from both sides. It's a partnership. We can't be like the lady that said, "Lord, I don't want anything for myself . . . just give mother a son-in-law!" It's got to be more than that. It's a partnership on the part of both individuals. You share and you share equally. You share the blessings and you share the burdens. It takes a strong commitment to establish a marriage based on a partnership relationship.

2. **Thou shalt be committed to a successful marriage.** You must have a commitment. You're going to have trials and you're going to have tribulations. You're not always going to see things alike. Only a strong commitment to succeed will prevail. Anyone can quit . . . it takes a winner to succeed! You have to have a commitment to turn your problems into projects. As long as you concentrate on the problems, you're never going to come up with the solutions. Go back and re-read the chapter on Problem Solving. You have to be **commited** to a successful marriage.

3. **Thou shalt be honest with each other.** Too many problems occur because the husband and wife are not honest with each other. They don't share their true feelings. Then feelings build up until an explosion occurs. You must be honest with each other. That's why they put a pressure valve on a steam

boiler . . . so it can release that pressure when necessary. You must be in a situation where you can communicate openly and honestly with your partner.

Dr. Fay once described nine of the most destructive habits which impair communications and sexual satisfaction among partners. Don't fall prey to these habits.

    a. Inattentiveness and lack of overt expression of interest in what the other person is saying. Insensitivities to the feelings and message of the partner.

    b. Bringing up past grievances . . . reciting past errors, misdeeds and dissatisfactions tends to destroy a relationship.

    c. Malignant hypothesis . . . drawing the wrong conclusion from a partner's behavior, such as feeling the partner is unhappy or angry with you if he or she doesn't go along with what you want.

    d. Insufficient positive reinforcement . . . the tendency to criticize your partner for things you don't like rather than saying what you do like.

    e. Labeling the other person . . . referring to your partner as a "sex maniac", a "pervert" or a "frigid woman".

f. Universalizing your own values and tastes . . . taking your views about sexual behavior or a given sexual practice to be right and good and assuming any other practice is automatically bad.

g. Using the absolute . . . like saying, "We **never** go out any more", or, "We **always** make love the same way", in a critical manner.

h. "You" messages . . . negative feelings are more apt to be destructive in a relationship if they start with "you" instead of "I".

i. Self-justification . . . blaming things that go wrong on your partner and and failing to look first at how "I" am contributing to the disharmony or what "I" can do to improve the situation.

Those nine destructive habits you should look at and analyze very carefully.

4. **Thou shalt be concerned about the other.** The Bible says our love for our neighbor should be as for ourselves. Then certainly our love for our spouse should be as great as it is for ourself. The Bible says that we shall leave our

father and our mother and become one flesh.

5. **Thou shalt set goals together.** Life is a goal-seeking opportunity. You may both have your personal goals, desires and objectives. But tied together with those will be joint goals, desires and objectives. It's much easier to achieve success and attain your goals by pulling together than it is by pulling apart.

6. **Thou shalt communicate your feelings.** You must set time aside each week to communicate your feelings. Don't tell your partner what you think . . . tell your partner what you feel.

7. **Thou shalt count your blessings, not your troubles.** I encourage you to sit down and make a list. On the left-hand side list all those things for which you should be thankful. On the right-hand side list those things which are problem areas for you. I'll guarantee that the list on the left . . . the list of blessings . . . will far outnumber the list of problems on the right.

8. **Thou shalt put yourself in the other person's shoes.** Joe South wrote a song entitled, "Walk A Mile In My Shoes."

> Hey, before you abuse,
> Criticize or accuse,
> Walk a mile in my shoes.

If you want your marriage to be based on the concepts of becoming Mental Millionaires, you must learn to see the world through the other person's eyes. Nowhere can I find in the marital ceremony where it says one must give up his soul . . . or one must give up his value structures. Those are yours and you have a right to them. Your partner must understand your individuality. You have the right to be an individual, but you must also appreciate the values and rights of your mate.

9. **Thou shalt build your marriage around God.** There's a saying that's been around for a long time--"The family that prays together, stays together." We defined love as a mental and physical attraction in the presence of emotional security, but there is also another key element to that relationship . . . the spiritual element. This is the ability to build your home around God. There will be times when you won't have the answers regardless of how hard you try. There will be times when you need spiritual guidance. I would highly recommend that you turn your life over to One who has the power, the understanding, and the compassion to lead you in the way you should go. It is better to light one candle than to curse the darkness, as we read in the Bible. So when you and I fail, or when you and I face situations that seem impossible, remember they are only impossible to us. With God, all things are possible!

10. **Thou shalt bring up your children in a Christian home.** The Bible says to bring up a child in the way he should go, and he will not

depart from it. You spend a great deal of money giving them clothing, giving them an education, and providing for their physical and mental needs. I encourage you to also provide for their spiritual needs. If you can plant within their minds the proper seeds, they will grow into the types of individuals you want them to become. A good illustration is this poem by Wilma Bergman.

One man plowed an open field and planted
winter wheat.
He labored for some months before the
harvest was complete.
Another wished his work to last his
lifetime through
And so he set a tree of oak and then, with
pride, he watched it grow.
Another planned eternity with manner
true and mild.
He placed a noble thought into the
heartstring of a child.

You and I have a responsibility to bring our children up in a Christian atmosphere.

While I very, very seldom use a negative approach to make a point, I encountered something several years ago that made a great impression on me. It was entitled, "Twenty-Five Ways To Make Your Child A Juvenile Delinquent." Let me share these with you, realizing that we will do the exact opposite of what is related here.

"25 Ways To Make Your Child A Juvenile Delinquent"

1. Don't give them religious training.

2. Don't respect women in front of them.

3. Never look for the cause of their lying.

4. Never take time to answer their questions.

5. Humiliate them in front of other people.

6. Don't reason with them . . . knock them down.

7. Disagree with your spouse. This confuses them.

8. Talk about guests just as soon as they leave.

9. Never explain anything. Make them guess.

10. Don't let them get an education.

11. Don't discuss their future.

12. Don't open your house to their friends.

13. Don't teach tolerance by example.

14. Don't give them an allowance. Force them to steal.

15. Blow up and never be calm.

16. Don't make a friend out of them.

17. Buy them expensive things and never teach them values.

18. Remind them every day how much they owe you.

19. Make the house a grouch nest.

20. Forget every promise you ever made to them.

21. Always accuse your daughter of being promiscuous.

22. Always leave the keys in the car.

23. Never praise them for their achievements.

24. Never tell them you love then.

25. Be a poor example.

Of course, you and I will do just the opposite. We want to see our children grow up with the proper seeds that will render the harvest we are looking for.

There is one other point I would like to make while talking about children and bringing them up in a Christian home and developing the right type of atmosphere. Never give your child special attention whey they are sick. Don't misunderstand me . . . I didn't say neglect them and I didn't say throw them out in the cold. What I am saying is that if you want to give your children special care or special attention, give it to them when they are well . . . because otherwise, if we only give them attention when they are ill, we will create a society of hypochondriacs.

Sometimes we get distorted values when we talk about marriage and raising our children. Naturally, we want the best for them, but what is the best? The best is to bring them up so they can have an understanding of the world in which they live, and so they are exposed to the spiritual values which can give them that peace that passeth all understanding. There are some things in life that fade and other things that remain constant. But, as the Bible says, "Heaven and earth shall pass away, but My Word shall not pass from you."

Nero was a great Emperor and Paul was a man imprisoned. But today, we call our dogs "Nero" and we call our sons "Paul." The following poem will help you to depict the advantages of bringing your child up in a Christian home. It will assist you in establishing the goals that are meaningful for your loved ones.

Now Jesus and Alexander
Both died at thirty-three.
One lived for self,
One died for you and me.

Love and Marriage

The Greek died on a throne.
The Jew died on a cross.
One had a life of triumph,
The other seemed a loss.

One led vast armies forth,
The other walked alone.
One shed a whole world's blood,
The other gave his own.

Yes, Jesus and Alexander
Both died at thirty-three.
One died at Babylon
And one at Calvary.

One man was all for himself,
And one himself he gave.
One conquered every throne,
The other every grave.

Yes, Jesus and Alexander
Both died at thirty-three.
The Greek made all men slaves
But the Jew made all men free.

The Greek forever dies,
The other forever lives.
For he loses all who gets
And wins all things who gives.

The secret of living is in **giving**. Make it your goal from this day forward to base your marriage on the principles of becoming Mental Million-aires. You must give! The Bible says, "As ye sow, so shall ye reap."

CHAPTER 11

HAVE AN EDUCATED HEART

"Keep thy heart with all diligence; for out of it are the issues of life."
Proverbs 4:23

"Create in me a clean heart, O God; and renew a right spirit within me." Psalms 51:10

You will notice the title of this chapter is "Have An Educated Heart." It doesn't say, "Get an education . . . and A.B. . . an M.S. . . or a Ph. D." It says, "Have an educated heart."

What is an educated heart? Basically, it means bringing happiness into someone's life. We meet so many people each day, and as Mental Millionaires you and I have a responsibility to spread sunshine and joy into some of those lives.

Life is like a journey
Taken on a train.
With a pair of travelers
At each window pane.

I may sit beside you
All the journey through,
Or I may sit elsewhere
Never knowing you.

But if fate should mark me
To sit by your side,
Let's be pleasant travelers . . .
It's so short a ride.

Have An Educated Heart

You and I live in the midst of a world of people. We are not individual islands. One of the
greatest attributes of becoming Mental Millionaires is our ability to be of service to mankind.
I never cease to be amazed at the reality of Jesus'
statement, "As ye sow, so shall ye reap." It
has been quoted throughout this book. I have
discovered in my lifetime that it is impossible
to outgive God.

> I count that day as wisely spent
> In which I do some good
> For someone who is far away
> Or shares my neighborhood.
>
> A day devoted to the deed
> That lends a friendly hand
> Demonstrates a willingness
> To care and understand.
>
> I long to be of usefulness
> In little ways and large
> Without a selfish motive
> And without the slightest charge.
>
> Because of my philosophy
> There never is a doubt
> That all of us are here on earth
> To help each other out.
>
> I feel the day is fruitful
> And the time is worth my while
> When I promote this happiness--
> One endearing smile.

A smile doesn't cost much . . . but it can spread a lot of sunshine into the lives of other people.

Have you ever done something for someone and they look at you with kindness and compassion . . . a big smile comes across their face, and they say, "Thank you." What a reward that is to the individual who has been of service to his fellow man! One of the greatest assets we can claim is the friendship that may exist in the life of someone else.

St. Francis of Assisi once prayed, "Lord, make me an instrument of thy peace. Where there is hate may I bring love. Where offense, may I bring pardon? May I bring union in place of discord? Truth replacing error. Faith where once there was doubt. Hope for despair. Light where once there was darkness. Joy to replace sadness. Make me not to so crave to be loved as to love. Help me to learn that in giving I may receive. In forgetting may I find life eternal."

One of the greatest rewards in becoming a Mental Millionaire is in having an educated heart.

> Count your garden by the flowers
> Never by the leaves that fall.
> Count your days by golden hours.
> Never look for clouds at all.
>
> Count your nights by stars, not shadows.
> Count your life by smiles, not tears.
> And then with joy on every birthday
> Count your age by friends--not years.

When we talk about having an educated heart,

Have An Educated Heart

there is one goal I would like for you to establish
as one of your own personal goals. Bring happiness into someone else's life! We live in a very
stingy world. We send flowers to people who
have stopped smelling . . . we say kind words to
people who have stopped hearing. If you have
words to speak in behalf of another, let them
be spoken when they can be enjoyed. Let them
be shared when they can be heard. If you have
a feeling to be expressed by flowers, let them
be sent when the fragrance can fill the nostrils
as well as the mind.

> Closed eyes cannot see the white roses,
> Cold hands cannot hold them you know,
> Breath that is stilled cannot gather
> The odors that sweet from them blow.
>
> Death with a peace beyond dreaming
> Its children of earth doth endow.
> Life is the time we can help them
> So give them the flowers now.
>
> Here are the struggles and strivings,
> Here are the cares and the tears.
> Now is the time to be smothering
> The frowns and the furls and the fears.
>
> What to closed ears are kind sayings?
> What to hushed hearts are deep vow?
> Naught can avail after parting,
> So give them the flowers now.

In the Bible it says that old men shall dream

dreams, and young men shall have visions. Our yesterdays, to many of us, are dreams, and hopefully our tomorrows are visions of virility and happiness. Today well-lived, will make every yesterday a dream of happiness and every tomorrow a vision of hope.

John Hall wrote a poem entitled, "At Day's End." With that poem I would like to close this chapter and close this book. As you look ahead, I hope you will be able to utilize some of the ideas I have shared with you in order that you might become a Mental Millionaire . . . that you might get more living out of life and more life out of living.

> Is anybody happier because you passed
> his way?
> Does anyone remember that you spoke
> to him today?
> The day is almost over and the toiling
> time is through,
> Is there anyone now to utter a kindly
> word of you?
>
> Can you say tonight in parting with
> the day that's slipping fast
> That you helped a single brother of the
> many that you passed?
> Is a single heart rejoicing over what you
> did or said?
> Does the man whose hopes were fading,
> now with courage look ahead?

Have An Educated Heart

Did you waste the day or lose it?
Was it well or sorely spent?
Did you leave a trail of kindness
Or a scar of discontent?

As you close your eyes in slumber
Do you think that God will say,
You have earned one more tomorrow
By the work you did today.

Recommended Readings

- Siddhartha by Hermann Hesse, www.bnpublishing.net

- The Anatomy of Success, Nicolas Darvas, www.bnpublishing.net

- The Dale Carnegie Course on Effective Speaking, Personality Development, and the Art of How to Win Friends & Influence People, Dale Carnegie, www.bnpublishing.net

- The Law of Success In Sixteen Lessons by Napoleon Hill (Complete, Unabridged), Napoleon Hill, www.bnpublishing.net

- It Works, R. H. Jarrett, www.bnpublishing.net

- The Art of Public Speaking (Audio CD), Dale Carnegie, wwww.bnpublishing.net

- The Success System That Never Fails (Audio CD), W. Clement Stone, www.bnpublishing.net

.

CPSIA information can be obtained
at www.ICGtesting.com
Printed in the USA
BVHW042024040720
582969BV00004B/647